新经典高等学校英语系列教程

丛书主编◎王立松　江滨　刘旸

U0960224

西方科幻文学选读

主编◎许谨　李彤　殷世宇

Selected Readings of Western Science Fiction Literature

天津大学出版社
TIANJIN UNIVERSITY PRESS

图书在版编目(CIP)数据

西方科幻文学选读：汉文、英文/ 许谨，李彤，殷世宇主编. -- 天津：天津大学出版社，2024. 11.
(新经典高等学校英语系列教程/ 王立松，江滨，刘旸主编). -- ISBN 978-7-5618-7794-4

Ⅰ. H319.37

中国国家版本馆CIP 数据核字第2024KK9674 号

XIFANG KEHUAN WENXUE XUANDU

依托项目：天津市普通高等学校本科教学改革与质量建设研究计划项目（项目编号：B231005613）

出版发行	天津大学出版社
地　　址	天津市卫津路92号天津大学内（邮编：300072）
电　　话	发行部：022-27403647
网　　址	www.tjupress.com.cn
印　　刷	廊坊市瑞德印刷有限公司
经　　销	全国各地新华书店
开　　本	787mm×1092mm　1/16
印　　张	10.75
字　　数	349千
版　　次	2024年11月第1版
印　　次	2024年11月第1次
定　　价	39.80元

前 言

随着时代的发展，高等学校英语教育正经历一场意义深远、影响深刻的变革。在这场变革中，我们不再仅仅聚焦于学生语言能力的提升，而是更加注重学生个人素养与人文精神的全面培育，旨在拓展其人文视野，培养出既拥有卓越语言综合运用能力，又具备跨文化交际能力、思辨创新能力的新时代复合型人才，以强化他们在全球化舞台上的核心竞争力。英语教学不仅能够从多个角度展现中西文化的经典瑰宝，还能够从诸多侧面深刻剖析当代社会的现实问题，为学生提供一条多元化、人文化、专业化的学习路径。正是基于这样的教育理念，“新经典高等学校英语系列教程”应运而生。

《西方科幻文学选读》作为“新经典高等学校英语系列教程”的关键组成部分，面向的是广大普通高等学校本科学生、英语专业学生和研究生，以及众多英语爱好者。它巧妙地将科幻文学融入英语学习之中，不仅全面锻炼学习者的听、说、读、写、译等语言技能，更在多重层面丰富了学习体验，激发了学习兴趣，促进了学习者综合素质的全面提升。

本教材具有如下主要特点。

内容丰富，经典再现。本书精选了西方科幻文学发展历程中不同阶段的代表性作家与作品，涵盖了从 19 世纪末至 20 世纪末的诸多经典之作。这些作品不仅映射出作者深邃的思想与非凡的创意，从更宽泛的意义上讲，更是代表了西方社会在不同时期对于未来、科技以及人类自身的深度思考。通过对赫伯特·乔治·威尔斯、艾萨克·阿西莫夫、布莱恩·奥尔迪斯等知名科幻作家经典文本的深入解读，学习者不仅能够领略到科幻文学的独特魅力，还能深入领会并欣赏科幻文学这一特殊的文学类型，同时借由这些作品洞悉不同时代的社会文化背景以及人类对未来的丰富想象。

词汇阅读，科幻特色。科幻文学当中蕴含着数量庞大的专业术语和新奇词汇。通过阅读科幻作品，学习者能够接触到这些词汇，进而拓展自己的词汇量。为了保障不同水平学习者阅读的顺畅性，本书在文旁注释、课后译文等细微之处进行了精心安排，以有效辅助文章的阅读。科幻文学往往牵涉科学、技术、哲学等多个领域，学习者能够通过科幻文学课程接触到跨学科的知识，促进学习者综合素质的全面提升。与此同时，复杂的情节和丰富的背景有利于增强学习者的理解能力和分析能力。

思维培养，能力创新。《西方科幻文学选读》绝非仅仅是一部简单的文学作品集，而是一个引领学习者勇闯未知领域的广阔平台。借由这些经典的科幻佳作，学习者能够于想象与现实之间觅得精妙的平衡，在科学与人文之间展开深邃的思索。科幻文学，作为一种独具特色的文学分支，不仅拥有极为丰富的想象力和强大的创造力，更具有对现实世界中社会、科技、伦理等诸多方面的深刻反省与犀利批判。每课主题均围绕科幻文学展开，鼓励学习者进行批判性分析与创新思维，培养他们对未来的大胆构想与对知识的无限渴望，助力他们养成终身学习的优良习惯。

实践贯通，学练结合。本书注重理论与实践的紧密结合，通过丰富多样、极具针对性的练习设置，巩固学生的英语学习成果。每个单元主题明确，两篇文章相辅相成，课后练习紧扣课文内容，旨在加深学习者对文章内涵的理解。同时，课前的引导性问题与课后的拓展问题，旨在锻炼学习者的口语表达与批判性思维能力。针对词汇的练习涉及构词法、词语搭配、单词辨识等内容，学练有机结合，成效更为显著。翻译练习突出中国特色和新时代特色，聚焦当代中国的发展与成就，阐释了中国道路和中国智慧。扫码听力、视听练习为学习者提供了便捷的学习途径，使随时随地学习成为现实。另外，每单元最后还有迷你百科，介绍更多科幻作家和他们的作品。

编者衷心希望，《西方科幻文学选读》能成为读者开启科幻文学世界的钥匙，引领大家领略科幻文学的无限魅力，激发对未来的无限想象，并从中获取对于当下社会的深刻启示。同时，也期待本书能成为读者进一步探究科幻文学及其相关主题的起始点，激发更多关于科技、伦理和人类未来的深度思考。在这个科技飞速发展的时代，科幻文学为我们提供了一份宝贵的思想利器，助力我们更好地理解和应对未来的挑战。在《西方科幻文学选读》的陪伴下，愿每一位读者都能在科幻的浩渺海洋中尽情遨游，探索未知，启迪智慧，成就非凡的自我。

编者

2024 年 6 月

Table of Contents

Unit 1

Herbert Wells and His *The Time Machine*

Starting out

Look at the pictures and discuss the following questions.

1. Do you think time is eternal?
2. Do you believe that there is a time machine in the world?
3. If you had a time machine, would you choose to go back to the past or go forward to the future?
4. If you had a time machine, which place would you most like to travel to?
5. If you had a time machine, which era would you most like to travel to?
6. Do you think time travel will come true in the future?

Part 1

Reading and Understanding

The Time Machine （Ⅰ）

1 The Time Traveller (for so it will be convenient to ***speak of** him) was **expounding** a **recondite** matter to us. His grey eyes shone and **twinkled**, and his usually pale face was **flushed** and **animated**. The fire burned brightly, and the soft radiance of the **incandescent lights** in the lilies of silver caught the bubbles that flashed and passed in our glasses. Our chairs, being his **patents**, embraced and **caressed** us rather than ***submitted to** be sat upon, and there was that luxurious after-dinner atmosphere when thought **roams** gracefully free of the **trammels** of ***precision**. And he put it to us in this way, marking the points with a lean forefinger, as we sat and lazily admired his **earnestness** over this new **paradox** (as we thought it) and his **fecundity**.

2 "You must follow me carefully. I shall have to ***controvert** one or two ideas that are almost universally accepted. The **geometry**, for instance, they taught you at school is founded on a **misconception**."

3 "Is not that rather a large thing to expect us to begin upon?" said Filby, an argumentative person with red hair.

4 "I do not ***mean to** ask you to accept anything without reasonable ground for it. You will soon admit as much as I need from you. You know of course that a mathematical line, a line of thickness ***nil**, has no real existence. They taught you that? Neither has a mathematical ***plane**. These things are mere abstractions."

5 "That is all right," said the Psychologist.

6 "Nor, having only length, breadth, and thickness, can a cube have a real existence."

7 "There I object," said Filby. "Of course a solid body may

speak of 谈论，谈及
expound 阐述，解释
recondite 深奥的
twinkle 发光，闪烁
flushed 脸红的
animated 有生气的
incandescent light 白炽灯
patent 专利，专利权
caress 爱抚，抚摸
submit to 屈服，服从
roam 漫步，漫游，闲逛
trammel 束缚，拘束
precision 准确性，精确性
earnestness 认真，诚挚
paradox 似是而非的论点
fecundity 多产
controvert 否认，驳斥
geometry 几何，几何学
misconception 错误想法
mean to 打算，有意做……
nil 无，零，不存在
plane 平面

exist. All real things — ”

8 “So most people think. But wait a moment. Can an ⋆**instantaneous** cube exist?”

9 “Don’t follow you,” said Filby.

10 “Can a cube that does not last for any time at all, have a real existence?”

11 Filby became **pensive**. “Clearly,” the Time Traveller ⋆**proceeded**, “any real body must have extension in four directions: it must have Length, Breadth, Thickness, and ⋆**Duration**. But through a natural ⋆**infirmity** of the flesh, which I will explain to you ⋆**in a moment**, we ⋆**incline to** overlook this fact. There are really four dimensions, three which we call the three planes of Space, and a fourth, Time. There is, however, a ⋆**tendency** to draw an unreal **distinction** between the former three dimensions and the latter, because it happens that our consciousness moves ⋆**intermittently** in one direction along the latter from the beginning to the end of our lives.”

12 “That,” said a very young man, making **spasmodic** efforts to relight his cigar over the lamp; “that ... very clear indeed.”

13 “Now, it is very remarkable that this is so extensively overlooked,” continued the Time Traveller, with a slight **accession** of cheerfulness. “Really this is what is meant by the Fourth Dimension, though some people who talk about the Fourth Dimension do not know they mean it. It is only another way of looking at Time. There is no difference between Time and any of the three dimensions of Space except that our consciousness moves along it. But some foolish people have ⋆**got hold of** the wrong side of that idea. You have all heard what they have to say about this Fourth Dimension?”

14 “I have not,” said the Provincial Mayor.

15 “It is simply this. That Space, as our mathematicians have it, is spoken of as having three dimensions, which one may call

instantaneous 瞬时的
pensive 沉思的，忧郁的
proceed 继续（做）
duration 持续
infirmity 体弱，疾病
in a moment 立刻，马上
incline to 倾向于
tendency 趋势，倾向
distinction 差别，区分
intermittently 间歇地
spasmodic 间接性的
accession 增加，加入
get hold of 领会，得到

Length, Breadth, and Thickness, and is always definable *by reference to three planes, each at right angles to the others. But some philosophical people have been asking why three dimensions particularly — why not another direction at right angles to the other three? — and have even tried to *construct a Four-Dimension geometry. Professor Simon Newcomb was expounding this to the New York Mathematical Society only a month or so ago. You know how on a flat surface, which has only two dimensions, we can represent a figure of a three-dimensional solid, and similarly they think that by models of three dimensions they could represent one of four — if they could master the perspective of the thing. See?"

16 "I think so," murmured the Provincial Mayor; and, knitting his brows, he *lapsed into an *introspective state, his lips moving as one who repeats mystic words. "Yes, I think I see it now," he said after some time, brightening in a quite transitory manner.

17 "Well, I do not mind telling you I have been at work upon this geometry of Four Dimensions for some time. Some of my results are curious. For instance, here is a portrait of a man at eight years old, another at fifteen, another at seventeen, another at twenty-three, and so on. All these are evidently sections, as it were, Three-Dimensional representations of his Four-Dimensioned being, which is a fixed and *unalterable thing."

18 "Scientific people," proceeded the Time Traveller, after the pause required for the proper *assimilation of this, "know very well that Time is only a kind of Space. Here is a popular scientific diagram, a weather record. This line I trace with my finger shows the movement of the barometer. Yesterday it was so high, yesterday night it fell, then this morning it rose again, and so gently upward to here. Surely the mercury did not trace this line in any of the dimensions of Space generally recognized?

by reference to 根据，依据
at right angles to 与……成直角
construct 构建，建造
perspective 透视法
murmur 低语，小声说
knit one's brows 皱眉
lapse into 陷入
introspective 反省的，内省的
mystic 神秘的
in a ... manner 以一种……的方式
transitory 短暂的，瞬变的
portrait 肖像
evidently 显然地，明显地
unalterable 不能改变的
assimilation 吸收，同化
barometer 气压计，晴雨表
mercury 汞，水银

But certainly it traced such a line, and that line, therefore, we must conclude was along the Time-Dimension."

19 "But," said the Medical Man, staring hard at a coal in the fire, "if Time is really only a fourth dimension of Space, why is it, and why has it always been, regarded as something different? And why cannot we move in Time as we move about in the other dimensions of Space?"

20 The Time Traveller smiled. "Are you sure we can move freely in Space? Right and left we can go, backward and forward freely enough, and men always have done so. I admit we move freely in two dimensions. But how about up and down? Gravitation limits us there."

21 "Not exactly," said the Medical Man. "There are balloons."

22 "But before the balloons, save for spasmodic jumping and the inequalities of the surface, man had no freedom of **vertical** movement."

23 "Still they could move a little up and down," said the Medical Man.

24 "Easier, far easier down than up."

25 "And you cannot move at all in Time, you cannot ***get away from** the present moment."

26 "My dear sir, that is just where you are wrong. That is just where the whole world has gone wrong. We are always getting away from the present movement. Our mental existences, which are immaterial and have no dimensions, are passing along the Time-Dimension with a **uniform velocity from the cradle to the grave**. Just as we should travel down if we began our existence fifty miles above the earth's surface."

27 "But the great difficulty is this," interrupted the Psychologist. "You can move about in all directions of Space, but you cannot move about in Time."

vertical 垂直的
get away from 远离，离开
uniform velocity 均速度
from the cradle to the grave 从生到死，一生

Developing Ideas

Task 1 Summarize the story and complete the table.

PARAS 1-10	The Time Traveller intended to explain something [1]__________ to people at a [2]__________ atmosphere. ● Mathematical [3]__________ are mere abstractions without real existence. ● A cube having only [4]__________ has no real existence.
PARAS 11-16	The Time Traveller introduced the concept of a fourth dimension — [5]__________. ● People overlooked the fact that [6]__________ moves along time intermittently. ● Time is not separated from the other three dimensions of space but is just another [7]__________ the fourth dimension. ● [8]__________ attempted to construct a four-dimensional geometry by models of [9]__________.
PARAS 17-27	The Time Traveller shared some of his curious findings: ● He presented portraits of a man at different ages as [10]__________ to show the fourth dimension does exist. ● He combined the changes of [11]__________ in the barometer with [12]__________ recording it to show time is only [13]__________. ● He corrected the wrong idea that [14]__________ and argued that the mental existences travel along [15]__________ with [16]__________ from birth to death. *Do you think it is possible to realize moving about in time?

Task 2 Decide whether the statements are true (T) or false (F) according to the passage.

☐ 1. The Time Traveller thought that all geometric knowledge students learned from the school was wrong.

☐ 2. The plane of Length is at the right angles to those of Breadth and Thickness.

☐ 3. It is impossible for people to prove the existence of the fourth dimension.

☐ 4. The Time Traveller believed that people can move freely in two dimensions because the gravitation limits.

☐ 5. The mental existence can move along Time Dimension because it is immaterial and has no dimensions.

☐ 6. The Psychologist, the Provincial Mayor, the Medical Man and Filby showed great curiosity about the topic in the discussion, but they still doubted about the time travel.

Using Language

Task 1 Complete the table with the correct form of the words given. Then complete the sentences with the correct form of the words in the table.

Verb	Noun	Adjective	Adverb
controvert			
	tendency		
	gravitation		
construct			
		introspective	
		unalterable	
	assimilation		
	precision		
	reference		
			intermittently

1. Our team ___________ feedback from customers to improve our product and meet their needs effectively.
2. The statement of the last witness ___________ the evidence of the first two, so the case was under further investigation.
3. The team engaged in a ___________ discussion to find a solution to the problem.
4. The watchmaker's high ___________ craftsmanship resulted in a timepiece that was both accurate and visually stunning.
5. The concept of ___________ totally changed our understanding of the universe.
6. If you live in this small town, you'll experience ___________ rain instead of continuous rain in spring.
7. The student included a comprehensive list of ___________ on the last page of his research paper.
8. ___________ on his past actions, he realized the mistakes he had made and the impact they had on others, driving him to seek forgiveness.
9. The law of nature, with its ___________ principles, ensures the balance and harmony of the natural world.
10. People ___________ procrastinate when faced with tasks they find challenging or uninteresting.

Task 2 Complete the sentences with the correct form of the phrases in the box.

speak of	submit to	in a moment	incline to
get hold of	lapse into	get away from	mean to

1. Jackson ___________ start exercising regularly and eating healthier to improve his overall well-being.
2. After a long and heated debate, she finally ___________ her opponent's arguments and conceded defeat.
3. Taking a vacation is the perfect way to recharge and ___________ the stresses of daily life.
4. During the meeting, she ___________ her concerns regarding the company's financial stability and suggested implementing cost-cutting measures to mitigate potential risks.
5. As the sun set, the once lively conversation ___________ an uncomfortable silence.
6. She ___________ believe in the power of positive thinking and its impact on personal growth.
7. I've been trying to ___________ my friend all day, but she hasn't been answering her phone.

8. The car came to a screeching halt ___________, narrowly avoiding a collision with the pedestrian.

Task 3 Translate the sentences into Chinese.

1. His grey eyes shone and twinkled, and his usually pale face was flushed and animated. The fire burned brightly, and the soft radiance of the incandescent lights in the lilies of silver caught the bubbles that flashed and passed in our glasses.

____

____

____

2. There is no difference between Time and any of the three dimensions of Space except that our consciousness moves along it. But some foolish people have got hold of the wrong side of that idea.

____

____

____

Task 4 Translate the paragraph into English.

文明因多样而交流，因交流而互鉴，因互鉴而发展。我们要加强世界上不同国家、不同民族、不同文化的交流互鉴，夯实共建亚洲命运共同体、人类命运共同体的人文基础。

中华文明是亚洲文明的重要组成部分。自古以来，中华文明在继承创新中不断发展，在应时处变中不断升华，积淀着中华民族最深沉的精神追求，是中华民族生生不息、发展壮大的丰厚滋养。中国的造纸术、火药、印刷术、指南针、天文历法、哲学思想、民本理念等在世界上影响深远，有力推动了人类文明发展进程。

（来源：习近平在亚洲文明对话大会开幕式上的主旨演讲《深化文明交流互鉴 共建亚洲命运共同体》）

Part 2

Appreciating and Comprehending

The Time Machine (Ⅱ)

1 The thing the Time Traveller held in his hand was a **glittering** metallic framework, scarcely larger than a small clock, and very delicately made. There was ivory in it, and some *****transparent** crystalline substance. And now I must be *****explicit**, for this that follows, unless his explanation is to be accepted, is an absolutely *****unaccountable** thing. He took one of the small *****octagonal** tables that were scattered about the room, and set it in front of the fire, with two legs on the **hearth rug**. On this table he placed the mechanism.

2 Then he drew up a chair, and sat down. The only other object on the table was a small shaded lamp, the bright light of which fell upon the model. There were also perhaps a dozen candles about, two in **brass candlesticks** upon the **mantel** and several in **sconces**, so that the room was brilliantly *****illuminated**. I sat in a low arm-chair nearest the fire, and I drew this forward so as to be almost between the Time Traveller and the fireplace. Filby sat behind him, looking over his shoulder. The Medical Man and the Provincial Mayor watched him in *****profile** from the right, the Psychologist from the left. The Very Young Man stood behind the Psychologist. We were all *****on the alert**. It appears incredible to me that any kind of trick, however *****subtly** *****conceived** and however **adroitly** done, could have been played upon us under these conditions.

3 The Time Traveller looked at us, and then at the mechanism. "Well?" said the Psychologist.

4 "This little affair," said the Time Traveller, resting his elbows upon the table and pressing his hands together above the **apparatus**, "is only a model. It is my plan for a machine to

glittering 辉煌的，闪闪发光的
transparent 透明的
explicit 明确表达的
unaccountable 难以解释的，不可理解的
octagonal 八边形的
hearth 火炉，壁炉
rug 毛毯，地毯，垫子
brass candlestick 铜烛台
mantel 壁炉架
sconce 烛台
illuminated 照亮的
profile 侧面
on the alert 警惕着
subtly 巧妙地
conceive 构思，设想
adroitly 熟练地，敏捷地
apparatus 器械，设备

travel through time. You will notice that it looks singularly **askew**, and that there is an odd twinkling appearance about this bar, as though it was in some way unreal." He pointed to the part with his finger. "Also, here is one little white **lever**, and here is another."

5 The Medical Man got up out of his chair and peered into the thing. "It's beautifully made," he said.

6 "It took two years to make," ***retorted** the Time Traveller. Then, when we had all imitated the action of the Medical Man, he said: "Now I want you clearly to understand that this lever, being pressed over, sends the machine **gliding into** the future, and this other reverses the motion. This **saddle** represents the seat of a time traveller. Presently I am going to press the lever, and off the machine will go. It will ***vanish**, pass into future Time, and disappear. Have a good look at the thing. Look at the table too, and satisfy yourselves there is no ***trickery**. I don't want to waste this model, and then be told I'm a **quack**."

7 There was a minute's pause perhaps. The Psychologist seemed about to speak to me, but changed his mind. Then the Time Traveller put forth his finger towards the lever. "No," he said suddenly. "Lend me your hand." And turning to the Psychologist, he took that individual's hand in his own and told him to put out his forefinger. So that it was the Psychologist himself who sent forth the model Time Machine on its ***interminable** voyage. We all saw the lever turn. I am absolutely certain there was no trickery. There was a breath of wind, and the lamp flame jumped. One of the candles on the mantel was **blown out**, and the little machine suddenly swung round, became ***indistinct**, was seen as a ghost for a second perhaps, as an **eddy** of faintly glittering brass and ivory; and it was gone, vanished! Save for the lamp the table was bare.

8 Everyone was silent for a minute. Then Filby said he was damned.

askew 歪斜的，歪的
lever 杠杆
retort 反驳
glide into 滑入
saddle 马鞍，车座
vanish 消失
trickery 诡计，欺骗
quack 江湖郎中，庸医
interminable 无止境的
blow out 吹灭，熄灭
indistinct 不清楚的
eddy 旋涡，涡流，逆流

9 The Psychologist recovered from his **stupor**, and suddenly looked under the table. At that the Time Traveller laughed cheerfully. "Well?" he said, with a **reminiscence** of the Psychologist. Then, getting up, he went to the tobacco jar on the mantel, and with his back to us began to fill his pipe.

10 We stared at each other. "Look here," said the Medical Man, "are you **in earnest** about this? Do you seriously believe that that machine has travelled into time?"

11 "Certainly," said the Time Traveller, **stooping** to **light a spill** at the fire. Then he turned, lighting his pipe, to look at the Psychologist's face. (The Psychologist, to show that he was not **unhinged**, helped himself to a cigar and tried to light it uncut.) "What is more, I have a big machine nearly finished in there" — he indicated the laboratory — "and when that is put together I mean to have a journey *****on my own account**."

12 "You mean to say that that machine has travelled into the future?" said Filby.

13 "Into the future or the past — I don't, for certain, know which."

14 After an interval the Psychologist had an inspiration. "It must have gone into the past if it has gone anywhere," he said.

15 "Why?" said the Time Traveller.

16 "Because I presume that it has not moved in space, and if it travelled into the future it would still be here all this time, since it must have travelled through this time."

17 "But," I said, "If it travelled into the past it would have been visible when we came first into this room; and last Thursday when we were here; and the Thursday before that; **and so forth**!"

18 "Serious objections," remarked the Provincial Mayor, with an air of **impartiality**, turning towards the Time Traveller.

19 "Not a bit," said the Time Traveller, and, to the Psychologist:

stupor 昏迷，恍惚
reminiscence 回忆，怀旧
in earnest 认真的，诚挚的
stoop 俯身，弯腰
light a spill 点燃一根纸捻
unhinged 精神错乱的
on one's own account 独自一人
and so forth 等等
impartiality 公平，公正

"You think. You can explain that. It's presentation **below the threshold**, you know, **diluted** presentation."

20 "Of course," said the Psychologist, and reassured us. "That's a simple point of psychology. I should have thought of it. It's plain enough, and helps the ★**paradox** delightfully. We cannot see it, nor can we appreciate this machine, any more than we can the spoke of a wheel spinning, or a bullet flying through the air. If it is travelling through time fifty times or a hundred times faster than we are, if it gets through a minute while we get through a second, the impression it creates will of course be only one-fiftieth or one-hundredth of what it would make if it were not travelling in time. That's plain enough." He passed his hand through the space in which the machine had been. "You see?" he said, laughing.

21 We sat and stared at the vacant table for a minute or so. Then the Time Traveller asked us what we thought of it all.

22 "It sounds ★**plausible** enough to-night," said the Medical Man; "but wait until tomorrow. Wait for the common sense of the morning."

23 "Would you like to see the Time Machine itself?" asked the Time Traveller. And **therewith**, taking the lamp in his hand, he led the way down the long, **draughty corridor** to his laboratory. I remember vividly the **flickering** light, his **queer**, broad head in **silhouette**, the dance of the shadows, how we all followed him, puzzled but ★**incredulous**, and how there in the laboratory we **beheld** a larger edition of the little mechanism which we had seen vanish from before our eyes. Parts were of **nickel**, parts of ivory, parts had certainly been **filed** or **sawn** out of **rock crystal**. The thing was generally complete, but the twisted crystalline bars lay unfinished upon the bench beside some sheets of drawings, and I took one up for a better look at it. **Quartz** it seemed to be.

below the threshold 低于阈值，低于门槛
diluted 无力的，稀释的
paradox 自相矛盾的人或事
plausible 似乎合理的
therewith 随即
draughty 通风的
corridor 走廊，过道
flickering 闪烁的，摇曳的
queer 奇怪的，异常的
silhouette 轮廓，侧影
incredulous 不轻信的
behold 目睹，看见
nickel 镍
file 锉平
saw 锯开
rock crystal 水晶石
quartz 石英

24 "Look here," said the Medical Man, "are you perfectly serious? Or is this a trick like that ghost you showed us last Christmas?"

25 "Upon that machine," said the Time Traveller, holding the lamp **aloft**, "I intend to explore time. Is that plain? I was never more serious in my life."

26 None of us quite knew how to take it.

27 I caught Filby's eye over the shoulder of the Medical Man, and he winked at me *****solemnly**.

aloft 在……之上
solemnly 严肃地

Developing Ideas

Task Work in groups and discuss the following questions.

1. What was the metallic framework that the Time Traveller held in his hand?
2. Did other people in the room believe the Time Traveller could make a machine to travel through time?
3. How many levers were there on the mechanism? What were their functions?
4. What precautions did the Time Traveller ask the others to take before he pressed the lever?
5. What happened to the machine when the lever was pressed?
6. Why couldn't people see the machine if it travelled to the past according to the passage?
7. What did the larger edition of the mechanism in the laboratory look like?

Using Language

Task 1 Learn the word formation from the table. Complete the sentences with the correct form of the words in the table.

Word	Prefix	Root	Suffix
octagonal	oct- 八	agon=angle	+al 形容词缀
transparent	trans- 越过	par 平等，相等	+ent ……的

Word	Prefix	Root	Suffix
interminable **indistinct** **incredulous**	in- 不，非，相反	termin 界限，末端 distinct 清楚的 cred 相信，信任	+able 能……的 / +ulous 多……的
illuminated	il- 使……进入	lumin 光	+ate 做，造成
conceive	con- 共同，一起	ceive 抓住，获取	/
explicit	ex- 出，出去	plic 重叠，折叠	+it 形容词缀
unaccountable	un- 否定前缀	account 解释	+able 能……的

1. The table in the conference room had an ___________ shape.
2. The meeting seemed ___________ as the speaker kept talking about the safety problem without any breaks.
3. The room was ___________ by the soft glow of the droplight, creating a warm and inviting atmosphere.
4. ___________ animals let light pass through their bodies the same way light passes through a window.
5. The sudden disappearance of the valuable artifact remains___________, leaving investigators puzzled.
6. The ___________ costs of attending college include tuition fees, textbooks, and housing expenses.
7. She could not ___________ of a scenario where her best friend betrayed her trust.
8. The figure in the distance was ___________, making it difficult to determine whether it was a person or a shadow.

Task 2 Complete sentences with the correct form of the words or phrases in the box.

subtly	retort	profile	on the alert
solemnly	vanish	paradox	on one's own account

1. The hikers remained ___________, scanning the surroundings for any signs of wildlife or potential dangers.
2. I decided to travel to Xizang ___________, seeking new experiences and personal growth.
3. Her impressive academic ___________ and extensive research experience made her a top candidate for the prestigious scholarship.

4. The judge ___________ declared the defendant guilty, emphasizing the seriousness of the crime committed.
5. After being accused of cheating, he defended himself with a well-reasoned argument that has been ___________ by his opponent.
6. Her version of events is ___________ different from what actually happened, which aroused the suspicion of the police.
7. The ___________ of love is that it can bring both immense joy and profound pain.
8. The magician performed a stunning trick, causing the coin to ___________ into thin air.

Task 3 Translate the paragraph into Chinese.

A Brief History of Time has become a landmark in popular science literature, captivating readers with its exploration of the universe's complexities and Hawking's engaging writing style. It provides a layman-friendly exploration of complex scientific concepts related to the universe and its origins. In around 200 pages, Stephen Hawking delves into topics like the nature of time, the Big Bang Theory, black holes, and the quest for a unified theory of everything. The book aims to make advanced theoretical physics accessible to the general reader. It covers a wide range of subjects, from the fundamental laws of physics to the intricacies of quantum mechanics and relativity. Hawking discusses how time is influenced by gravity, the nature of singularities(奇点) within black holes, and the challenges of merging quantum mechanics with general relativity. Throughout the book, Hawking emphasizes the importance of understanding these ideas in a broader context and encourages readers to contemplate the profound questions they raise. He also touches on the anthropic principle(人择原理), which suggests that the universe's physical constants are finely tuned to allow for life. *A Brief History of Time* serves as a window into the mysteries of the cosmos for those without a formal scientific background.

Part 3

Watching, Listening and Doing

Watching and Doing

SCAN ME!

Task 1 Scan the QR code to watch the video clip "The Life Story of H. G. Wells (Ⅰ)" and fill in the blanks.

Herbert George Wells, commonly known as H. G. Wells, was a prolific English writer and one of the [1]__________ of science fiction. Born on September 21, 1866, in Bromley, Kent, England, Wells had a profound impact on the genre and left an indelible mark on literature as a whole.

Wells grew up in a [2]__________ family and faced financial struggles throughout his early life. Despite these challenges, he displayed a remarkable intellect and a passion for learning. Wells won a [3]__________ to study at the prestigious Normal School of Science (now the Royal College of Science) in London, where he developed a deep interest in [4]__________ and the natural sciences. This scientific background would later influence his writing, as he often [5]__________ scientific concepts and theories into his works.

Wells began his writing career as a [6]__________, working for various newspapers and magazines. However, it was his first attempt at fiction that would bring him widespread recognition. In [7]__________, he published his first novel, *The Time Machine*, which earned him literary fame. The novel introduced the concept of time travel and explored themes of social class, [8]__________, and the potential future of humanity. It was an instant success and established Wells as a leading figure in the [9]__________ genre of science fiction.

SCAN ME!

Task 2 Scan the QR code to watch the video clip "The Life Story of H. G. Wells (Ⅱ)" and fill in the blanks.

Following the success of *The Time Machine*, Wells continued to produce [1]__________ influential and groundbreaking works. In 1897, he published *The Invisible Man*, a story about a scientist who discovers a way to make himself invisible but [2]__________ the consequences of his newfound power. This novel aimed to find out themes of identity, morality, and the dangers of unchecked scientific progress.

Wells further [3]__________ his reputation as a master of science fiction with the publication of *The War of the Worlds* in 1898. This novel [4]__________ an alien invasion of Earth and explored themes of imperialism, human resilience, and the fragility of civilization. *The War of the*

Worlds remains one of Wells' most famous and [5]____________ works, inspiring numerous adaptations in various media.

Beyond science fiction, Wells also wrote in other genres, including history, politics, and social criticism. He was a vocal advocate for [6]____________ and used his writing to address pressing issues of his time. Wells wrote extensively on topics such as socialism, women's rights, and the dangers of war. His non-fiction works, such as *Anticipations* and *The Outline of History*, showcased his [7]____________ thinking and his ability to analyze and predict future societal developments.

Wells' writing style was characterized by [8]____________ adventure, social commentary, and scientific speculation. He had a knack for creating vivid and imaginative worlds, often using his stories as a vehicle to explore complex ideas and challenge societal norms. Wells' works were not only entertaining but also [9]____________, encouraging readers to contemplate the consequences of scientific advancements and the potential future of humanity.

H. G. Wells' [10]____________ literature and science fiction cannot be overstated. His works have had a [11]____________ on popular culture, inspiring countless authors, filmmakers, and artists. Wells' ideas and concepts continue to be explored and adapted in various forms of media, cementing his status as one of the most influential writers of his time.

Herbert George Wells passed away on August 13, 1946, [12]____________ a rich and diverse body of work that continues to captivate readers and shape the landscape of science fiction. His [13]____________ as a visionary writer and social commentator remains as relevant today as it was during his lifetime.

Listening and Doing

Task ***Scan the QR code to listen to the audio clip "Time Machines" and decide whether the statements are true (T) or false (F).***

SCAN ME!

1. The idea of traveling through time has attracted and delighted humanity for centuries.
2. The concept of time travel has only been explored in literature and popular culture.
3. In his novel, Wells embarked on a journey to the distant future as a Time Traveller.
4. Time travel may allow us to have the opportunity to witness historical events firsthand.
5. Time travel may raise ethical and philosophical questions because of its uncertainties.
6. Time machines have been successfully invented and continue to captivate our imagination.

Further Reading

Mini-Pedia — About "Time Travel"

Apart from H. G. Wells, there are two other writers who explore the same futuristic concepts: time travel.

George R. R. Martin (1948-), born on September 20, 1948, is an American author renowned for his epic fantasy series, *A Song of Ice and Fire*. Hailing from Bayonne, New Jersey, Martin developed a passion for storytelling at a young age. He began his writing career in the 1970s, crafting numerous short stories and novels in the science fiction, fantasy, and horror genres.

However, Martin's most notable work is undoubtedly the *A Song of Ice and Fire* series, which has captivated readers worldwide. Known for its intricate plotlines, morally complex characters, and realistic portrayal of political intrigue and warfare, the series has garnered immense popularity and critical acclaim. His book *The Dying of the Light* explores the concept of time travel as the protagonist embarks on a journey through different eras, unraveling the mysteries of the universe. With Martin's signature storytelling and intricate world-building, this time travel tale is a captivating and thought-provoking addition to his repertoire.

Martin's richly detailed world-building and unpredictable narrative have made him one of the most influential and celebrated authors of our time. Despite the long gaps between his books, Martin's contributions to the fantasy genre have solidified his status as a master storyteller.

Audrey Niffenegger (1963-) is an acclaimed American author and visual artist known for her unique blend of literary fiction and fantastical elements. Born on June 13, 1963, in South Haven, Michigan, Niffenegger developed a passion for storytelling and art from a young age. She pursued her artistic interests by studying visual arts, printmaking, and book arts, eventually earning a Master of Fine Arts degree from Northwestern University.

Niffenegger gained widespread recognition with her debut novel, *The Time Traveler's Wife*, published in 2003. This captivating love story revolves around the complex relationship between Henry, a man with a genetic disorder that causes him to time travel involuntarily, and Clare, his wife. The novel's intricate narrative structure and emotional depth resonated with readers worldwide, earning it critical acclaim and commercial success. It was later adapted into a film in 2009.

Known for her unique blend of romance, science fiction, and fantasy, Niffenegger's writing often explores themes of love, loss, and the complexities of human relationships. She has also published other works, including *Her Fearful Symmetry* and *The Night Bookmobile*, and has continued to create visual art alongside her writing career. Niffenegger's imaginative storytelling and ability to blend genres have made her a beloved and influential figure in contemporary literature.

Answer

Unit 2

John Steinbeck and His Human History

Starting out

Look at the pictures and discuss the following questions.

1. What do you know about the Neolithic Age (New Stone Age)?
2. What tools could Neolithic humans use?
3. What stimulated the beginning of farming and commerce in the Neolithic Age?
4. How did primitive tribes develop into city-states?
5. Do you know anything about the cultural relics of the Neolithic age in China and other countries?

Part 1

Reading and Understanding

The Primitive Life

1 It was pretty draughty in the cave in the middle of the afternoon. There wasn't any fire — the last spark had *gone out six months ago and the family wouldn't have any more fire until lightning struck another tree.

2 Joe came into the cave all scratched up and some hunks of hair *torn out and he flopped down on the wet ground and bled — Old William was arguing away with Old Bert who was his brother and also his son, if you look at it one way. They were quarrelling *mildly over a *spoiled chunk of mammoth meat.

3 Old William said, "Why don't you give some to your mother?"

4 "Why?" asked Old Bert. "She's my wife, isn't she?"

5 And that finished that, so they both took after Joe.

6 "Where's Al" one of them asked and the other said, "You forgot to roll the rock in front of the door."

7 Joe didn't even look up and the two old men agreed that kids were going to the devil. "I tell you it was different in my day," Old William said. "They had some respect for their elders or they got what for."

8 After a while Joe stopped bleeding and he caked some mud on his cuts. "Al's gone," he said.

9 Old Bert asked brightly, "Sabre tooth?"

10 "No, it's that new bunch that moved into the copse down the gully. They ate Al."

11 "*Savages," said Old William. "Still live in trees. They aren't *civilized. We don't hardly ever eat people."

12 Joe said, "We hardly got anybody to eat except relatives and we're getting low on relatives."

go out 熄灭
scratch up 刮伤
hunk 大片，大块
tear out 撕下，撕掉
flop down 突然疲惫地坐下或倒下
mildly 轻微地，温和地
spoiled 腐坏的
chunk 大块，厚块
mammoth 猛犸象
go to the devil 堕落，滚开
cake 覆盖
sabre tooth 剑齿虎
bunch 一群，一伙
copse 小灌木丛
gully 沟壑，溪谷
savage 野蛮人
civilized 文明的，开化的
get low on 变少

13 "Those foreigners!" said Old Bert.

14 "Al and I dug a **pit**," said Joe. "We caught a horse and those tree people came along and ate our horse. When we complained, they ate Al."

15 "Well, you go right out and get us one of them and we'll eat him," said Old William.

16 "Me and who else?" said Joe. "Last time it was warm there was twelve of us here. Now there's only four. **Why**, I saw my own sister Sally sitting up in a tree with a savage. Had my heart set on Sally, too, Pa," Joe went on uncertainly, because Old William was not only his father, but his uncle and his first and third cousin, and his brother-in-law. "Pa, why don't we **join up with** those tree people? They've got a net kind of thing — catch all sorts of animals. They eat better than we do."

17 "Son," said Old William, "they're foreigners, that's why. They live in trees. We can't ⋆**associate with** savages. How'd you like your sister to marry a savage?"

18 "She did!" said Joe. "We could have them come and live in our cave. Maybe they'd show us how to use that net thing."

19 "Never," said Old Bert. "We couldn't trust them. They might eat us in our sleep."

20 "If we didn't eat them first," said Joe. "I sure would like to have me a nice **juicy** piece of savage right now. I'm hungry."

21 "Next thing you know, you'll be saying those tree people are as good as us," said Old William. "I never saw such a boy. Why, where'd ⋆**authority** be? Those foreigners would take over. We'd have to ⋆**look up to** 'em. They'd ⋆**outnumber** us."

22 "I hate to tell you this, Pa," said Joe. "I've got a **busted** arm. I can't dig pits any more — neither can you. You're too old. Bert can't either. We've got to **merge up** with those tree people or we aren't gonna eat anything or anybody."

23 "Over my dead body," said Old William, and then he saw

pit 坑
why 惊讶或不耐烦时发出的感叹
join up with 与……结合在一起
associate with 与……交往，联系
juicy 多汁的
authority 权威，当权者
look up to 尊敬
outnumber（数量上）压倒
bust 打破，摔碎
merge up 合并

Joe's eyes on his **skinny flank** and he said, "Now, Joe, don't you go getting ideas about your Pa."

㉔Well, a long time ago before the tribe first moved out of the **drippy** cave, there was a man named Elmer. He piled up some rocks in a circle and laid **brush** on top and took to living there. The elders killed Elmer **right off**. If anybody could go off and live by himself, why, where would authority be? But pretty soon those elders moved into Elmer's house and then the other families made houses just like it. It was pretty nice with no water dripping in your face.

㉕So, they made Elmer a god — used to ****swear*** by him. Said he was the moon.

㉖Everything was going along fine when another tribe moved into the valley. They didn't have Elmer houses, though. They **shacked up** in skin tents. But you know, they had a funny kind of a **gadget** that shot little sticks ... shot them a long way. They could just stand still and **pick off** a pig, oh ... fifty yards away — wouldn't have to run it down and maybe get a **tusk** in the **groin**.

㉗ The skin tribe shot so much **game** that naturally the Elmer elders said those savages had to be got rid of. They didn't even know about Elmer — that's how ***ignorant** they were. The old people sharpened a lot of sticks and fired the points and they said, "Now you young **fellas** go out and **drive** those skin people **away**. You can't fail because you've got Elmer on your side."

㉘Now, it seems that a long time ago there was a skin man named Max. He ***thought up** this stick **shooter** so they killed him, naturally, but afterwards they said he was the sun. So, it was a war between Elmer, the moon, and Max, the sun, but in the course of it **a whole slew of** young skin men and a whole slew of young Elmer men got killed. Then a forest fire broke out and drove the game away. Elmer people and skin people had to

skinny 皮包骨的
flank 肋腹
drippy 潮湿的
brush 灌木丛
right off 马上
swear 发誓
shack up 同居，居住
gadget 小器具
pick off 瞄准射死，摘下
tusk 长牙
groin 腹股沟
game 猎物
ignorant 无知的，愚昧的
fella 小伙子
drive away 赶走
think up 发明
shooter 射击武器
a whole slew of 大量的

* **make for** the hills all together. The elders of both tribes never would accept it. They complained until they died.

29 You can see from this that the world started **going to pot** right from the beginning. Things would be going along fine — law and order and all that and the elders in charge — and then some **smart aleck** would invent something and spoil the whole business — like the man Ralph who forgot to kill all the wild chickens he caught and had to build a hen house, or like the real trouble-maker Jojo **au front du chien**, who patted some seeds into **damp** ground and invented farming. Of course, they tore Jojo's arms and legs off and rightly so because when people plant seeds, they can't **go golly-wacking** around the country enjoying themselves. When you've got a crop in, you stay with it and get the weeds out of it and harvest it. Furthermore, everything and everybody wants to take your crop away from you, — weeds, bugs, birds, animals, men. A farmer spends all his time **fighting** something **off**. The elders can **call on** Elmer all they want, but that won't keep the neighbours from over the hill out of your corn **crib**.

make for 向……走去
go to pot 走下坡路
smart aleck 自作聪明的人
au front du chien（法语）在狗的前面，这里有先于别人尝试做某事之意
damp 潮湿的
go golly-wacking（非正式表达）通常用于描述某人或某物在不负责任或不受约束地行动
fight off 击退，战胜
call on 呼吁，要求
crib 饲料槽，粮仓

Developing Ideas

Task 1 Summarize the story and complete the table.

PARAS 1-23	1 ____________ of the family living in the cave. The elders 2 ____________ the foreigners, because they believed that: a. These new comers were 3 ____________ for they lived in trees; b. The 4 ____________ tree people would 5 ____________; c. The foreigners 6 ____________ the family, so they would take over their authority.

PARAS 24-28	Elmer devised [7] ____________ while Max invented [8] ____________. ● About the fight: Elmer ([9] ____________) vs [10] ____________(the sun). ● Cause: The skin tribe shot so much [11] ____________. ● Reasons why they stopped fighting: a. A large number of [12] ____________ died in [13] ____________ tribes; b. [14] ____________ broke out. ● Results: [15] ____________.
PARA 29	Some [16] ____________ such as livestock rearing and [17] ____________ as new lifestyles broke the existing [18] ____________ and promoted the social development. *Compared with their primitive antecedents who lived in caves, people at this stage began to establish civilization. What other inventions could improve human development? What would happen at the next stage?

Task 2　Decide whether the statements are true (T) or false (F) according to the passage.

☐ 1. Al did not return with Joe because he was killed by a sabre tooth.

☐ 2. Old William and Old Bert were willing to live with those tree people.

☐ 3. The elders killed Elmer for he could make a house with rocks, brush and skins.

☐ 4. Elmer was called the moon while Max was addressed as the sun.

☐ 5. The skin tribe could stand still to kill a pig fifty yards away.

☐ 6. The forest fire made the two tribes fight against each other.

Using Language

Task 1　Complete the sentences with the correct form of the words in the table.

mildly	civilized	savage	outnumber
ignorant	authority	spoil	swear

1. From the terrible and hopeless condition of being a naked ____________, man has risen to

command the earth.

2. It is up to the ___________ to put the measures into effect and regulate them.
3. He ___________ all the "No Smoking" signs and the persuasions from others, lighting up a cigarette.
4. As the boat swung ___________ and waves sounded pleasant, the children got asleep very soon.
5. It is believed that without unwritten rules, ___________ life would be impossible.
6. Grandparents are often tempted to ___________ their grandchildren whenever they come to visit.
7. There is gender discrimination in workplace, and men still ___________ women in the paid workforce.
8. You have ___________ to tell the truth, otherwise you would be held legally responsible.

Task 2 Complete the sentences with the correct form of the phrases in the box.

merge up	tear out	look up to
think up	go out	associate with

1. To deal with the challenge, some large iron enterprises started to ___________.
2. Reform is to resolutely give up the old ways and courageously ___________ new ones.
3. Many successful people choose to ___________ individuals who inspire and motivate them to achieve their goals.
4. My father certainly has great influence on me and I always ___________ him.
5. As a flash of lightning struck, the bedroom light ___________ after a short moment.
6. He was punished because he ___________ some pages after reading the book in the library.

Task 3 Translate the sentences into Chinese.

1. Joe came into the cave all scratched up and some hunks of hair torn out and he flopped down on the wet ground and bled — Old William was arguing away with Old Bert who was his brother and also his son, if you look at it one way.

____

____

2. Things would be going along fine — law and order and all that and the elders in charge — and then some smart aleck would invent something and spoil the whole business — like the man Ralph who forgot to kill all the wild chickens he caught and had to build a hen house, or like the real trouble-maker Jojo au front du chien, who patted some seeds into damp ground and invented farming.

____

____

____

____

____

____

Task 4　Translate the paragraph into English.

中国要建设的现代化，是人口规模巨大、全体人民共同富裕、物质文明和精神文明相协调、人与自然和谐共生、走和平发展道路的现代化，我们决不会通过战争、殖民、掠夺(plunder)等方式实现现代化，一定会用和平和发展的方式使14亿多人口整体迈进现代化社会，这将为亚洲和世界经济增长带来强劲动能(impetus)。完成这个中心任务，需要长时间的持续奋斗。在这个过程中，不论世界发生什么样的变化，我们都将始终坚持改革开放、创新驱动，既为整个世界经济发展不断注入新的动力和活力，也让世界各国分享中国发展的机遇和红利。我想，一个长期稳定、一心发展的中国，一个脚踏实地、勇毅前行的中国，一个自信开放、乐于共享的中国，一定是世界繁荣稳定的巨大力量。

(来源：国务院总理李强在博鳌亚洲论坛二〇二三年年会开幕式上的主旨演讲《以人类命运共同体理念为引领 为世界和平与发展注入更多确定性》)

Part 2

Appreciating and Comprehending

The Neolithic Age

1 Well, there was a strong boy named Rudolph, but called Bugsy. Bugsy would break his back **wrestling** but he wouldn't bring in an **armload** of wood. Bugsy just naturally liked to fight and he hated to work, so he said, "You men just plant your crops and don't worry. I'll take care of you. If anybody bothers you, I'll **clobber** 'em. You can give me a few chickens and a couple of ★**handfuls of grits** for my trouble."

2 The elders blessed Bugsy and pretty soon they got him mixed up with Elmer. Bugsy ★**went** right **along with** them. He gathered a dozen strong boys and built a **fort** up on the hill to take care of those farmers and their crops. When you take care of something, pretty soon you own it.

3 Bugsy and his boys would **stroll** around picking over the crop of wheat and girls and when they worked over their own valley, they'd go **rollicking** over the hill to see what the neighbours had ★**stored up** or born. Then the strong boys from over the hill would come rollicking back and what they couldn't carry off they burned until pretty soon it was more dangerous to be protected than not to be. Bugsy took everything loose up to his fort to protect it and very little ever came back down. He figured his grandfather was Elmer now and that made him different from other people. How many people do you know that have the moon in their family?

4 By now the elders had ★**confused** protection **with** virtue because Bugsy **passed out** his **surplus** to the better people. The elders ★**were** pretty **hard on** anybody who complained. They said it was a **sin**. Well, the farmers built a wall around the hill to sit in when the going **got rough**. They hated to see their crops

wrestle 摔跤
armload 一抱之量
clobber 击倒
a handful of 一把
grits 玉米粉
go along with 遵守，服从
fort 堡垒
stroll 闲逛
rollicking 喧闹嬉戏的
store up 存储
confuse ... with ... 将……与……混淆
pass out 分发
surplus 剩余
be hard on 对……严苛
sin 罪恶
get rough 变得困难

burn up, but they hated worse to see themselves burn up and their wife Agnes and their daughter Clarinda.

5 About that time the whole system **turned over**. Instead of Bugsy protecting them, it was their duty to protect him. He said he got the idea from Elmer one full-moon night.

6 People spent a lot of time sitting behind the wall waiting for the smoke to clear and they began to ★**fool around with** willows from the river, making baskets. And it's natural for people to make more things than they need.

7 Now, it happens often enough so that you can make a rule about it. There's always going to be a joker. This one was named Harry and he said, "Those ignorant pigs over the hill don't have any willows so they don't have any baskets, but you know what they do? — ★**benighted** though they are, they take mud and pat it out and put it in the fire and you can boil water in it. I'll bet if we took them some baskets they'd give us some of those baked mud pots." They had to hang Harry head down over a **bonfire**. Nobody can put a knife in the **status quo** and **get away with** it. But it wasn't long before the basket people got to **sneaking** over the hill and coming back with pots. Bugsy tried to stop it and the elders were right with him. It took people away from the fields, **exposed** them to dangerous ideas. Why, pots got to be like money and money is worse than an idea. Bugsy himself said, "Makes folks ★**restless** — why, it makes a man think he's as good as the ones that got it a couple of generations earlier" and how's that for being un-Elmer? The elders agreed with Bugsy, of course, but they couldn't stop it, so they all had to join it. Bugsy took half the pots they brought back and pretty soon he took over the willow **concession** so he got the whole thing.

8 About then some savages moved up on the hill and got to **raiding** the basket and pot trade. The only thing to do was for

turn over 翻转
fool around with 玩弄
benighted 愚昧的
bonfire 篝火
status quo 现状
get away with （做坏事而）未受惩罚
sneak 偷偷地走，溜
expose 使面临，使遭受（危险或不快）
restless 不安的
concession 经营权
raid 抢劫

Bugsy, the basket, to marry the daughter of Willy, the pot, and when they all died off, Herman Pot-Basket pulled the whole business together and made a little state and that worked out fine.

9 Well, it went on from state to league and from league to nation. (A nation usually had some kind of natural *boundary like an ocean or a mountain range or a river to keep it from spilling over.) It worked out fine until a bunch of jokers invented long-distance stuff like **directed missiles** and **atom bombs**. Then a river or an ocean didn't do a bit of good. It got too dangerous to have separate nations just as it had been to have separate families.

10 When people are finally faced with *extinction, they have to do something about it. Now we've got the United Nations and the elders are right there fighting it the way they fought coming out of caves. But we don't have much choice about it. It isn't any **goodness** of heart and we may not want to go ahead but right from the cave time we've had to choose and so far we've never chosen extinction. It'd be kind of silly if we killed ourselves off after all this time. If we do, we're stupider than the cave people and I don't think we are. I think we're just exactly as stupid and that's pretty bright in the long run.

boundary 边界
directed missiles 定向导弹
atom bomb 原子弹
extinction 灭绝
goodness 善良，美德

Developing Ideas

Task ***Work in groups and discuss the following questions.***

1. Why would Bugsy like to protect the farmers?
2. What new lifestyle emerged in the Neolithic age?
3. Why was it more dangerous to be protected than not to be?
4. Why did Bugsy regard Elmer as his grandfather?
5. Can you explain how the willow business evolved?
6. Is there any stupid choice humans have made in contemporary era?

Using Language

Task 1 Learn the word formation from the table. Complete the sentences with the correct form of the words in the table.

Word	Prefix	Root	Suffix
handful	/	hand 手	+ful 充满……时的量，名词缀
benighted	be- 加强或引申意义	night 夜晚	+ed ……的，形容词缀
restless	/	rest 休息	+less 无……的，形容词缀
concession **extinction**	con- 共同，一起 ex- 出，向外	cess 行走，退让 (s)tinct 刺，扑灭	+sion/+tion, 名词缀，表示行为、过程或结果
boundary	/	bond 形成……的边界	+ary 名词缀，表示场所、地点

1. For nearly 30 years from independence in 1975 Angola was involved in civil war and known as one of the most ____________ places in the world.
2. The fence marked the ____________ between my property and hers to avoid further troubles.
3. When different ideas appear, I might make a little ____________ to avoid dispute.
4. As the years passed, he began to get a little ____________ in his forties.
5. I hate measuring, and I say things like a pinch of salt, a ____________ of flour, some of this and a splosh of that.
6. It is unbelievable that many species have been shot to the verge of ____________.

Task 2 Complete the sentences with the correct form of the phrases in the box.

go along with	confuse ... with	be hard on
fool around with	get away with	store up

1. She thought she could ____________ cheating on the exam, but the teacher caught her in the act.
2. To the general public, depression can be easily ____________ stress, as it may be a response to some types of stress.
3. For most entrepreneurs, the first few years of business can ____________ them and their family.
4. My friends asked me about how much toilet paper they should ____________ for emergency use.

5. If I were a member of your company, I would ____________ your company policy and pay scale.
6. We'd better treat our earth in a friendly way and never ____________ mother nature.

Task 3 Translate the paragraph into Chinese.

Asia is home to one of the earliest human settlements and an important cradle of human civilizations. This vast and beautiful continent covers a third of the earth's land mass and has two-thirds of the world's population ... For several thousand years before the Common Era, our forefathers living along ... the Yellow River and the Yangtze, tilled and irrigated the land, made tools and utensils, and built homes to live in. Generation after generation, our ancestors in Asia, with their tireless endeavors, created a time-honored history and profound and rich civilizations. Our vast and fertile plains, beautiful river basins, large steppes, immense deserts, mighty rivers and oceans, and lofty mountains have nourished and enriched diverse and colorful civilizations across Asia.

We Asian countries are closely connected and share a natural bond of affinity. We went through similar historical trials and hold the same dream for the future. Going forward, we need to see where the world is going, ride on the trend of the times and turn our people's longing for a better life into reality.

(A keynote speech "Deepening exchanges and mutual learning among civilizations for an Asian community with a shared future" delievered by Xi Jinping at the opening ceremony of the Conference on Dialogue of Asian Civilizations)

Watching, Listening and Doing

Part 3

Watching and Doing

Task 1 Scan the QR code to watch the video clip "The Story of John Steinbeck (Ⅰ)" and fill in the blanks.

SCAN ME!

John Steinbeck is widely regarded as one of the most [1]____________ American writers of the 20th century. Born on February 27, 1902, in Salinas, California, Steinbeck grew up in a region that would later serve as the [2]____________ for many of his novels. His works often explore themes of social justice, the plight of the [3]____________ class, and the human condition. Steinbeck's writing style is characterized by its vivid descriptions, [4]____________ dialogue, and successful character shaping. His ability to capture the [5]____________ of the human experience and shed light on important social issues has made his works timeless. Steinbeck's writing often prompts discussions on topics such as poverty, [6]____________, the American Dream, and the power of resilience.

Steinbeck attended Stanford University in the 1920s but did not graduate. Instead, he [7]____________ a career as a freelance writer, working odd jobs to himself. During this time, he traveled extensively, which provided him with [8]____________ experiences and inspiration for his later works. His first novel, *Cup of Gold*, was published in 1929, but it was his later works that brought him widespread acclaim.

Task 2 Scan the QR code to watch the video clip "The Story of John Steinbeck (II)" and fill in the blanks.

SCAN ME!

One of Steinbeck's most [1]____________ novels is *The Grapes of Wrath*, published in 1939. Set during the Great Depression, the novel follows the Joad family as they [2]____________ from Oklahoma to California in search of a better life. Through their struggles and hardships Steinbeck explores themes of poverty, inequality, and the resilience of the human spirit. *The Grapes of Wrath* won the Pulitzer Prize for Fiction in [3]____________ and solidified Steinbeck's reputation as a master storyteller.

Another notable work by Steinbeck is *Of Mice and Men*, published in 1937. This novella tells the story of George Milton and Lennie Small, two displaced ranch workers in California during the Great [4]____________. The book delves into themes of friendship, dreams, and the [5]____________ loneliness of the experience. *Of Mice and Men* has become a staple in many high school and college curricula due to its [6]____________ language and powerful exploration of universal themes.

Steinbeck's other works include *East of Eden* (1952), *Cannery Row* (1945), and *Travels with Charley: In Search of America* (1962). *East of Eden* is an [7]____________ family saga set at the Salinas Valley, drawing inspiration from the biblical story of Cain and Abel. Cannery Row is a [8]____________ and poignant [9]____________ of life in a small coastal town in Monterey, California. *Travels with Charley* is a nonfiction account of Steinbeck's road trip across America with his poodle, Charley, providing a unique [10]____________ on the American landscape and its people.

In addition to his literary contributions, Steinbeck was also a political activist. He used his platform to advocate for the rights of workers and the disenfranchised (被剥夺公民权的人). His experiences during the Great Depression and witnessing the hardships faced by [11]____________ greatly influenced his political beliefs and writing.

John Steinbeck's impact on American literature cannot be [12]____________. His ability to create vivid, relatable characters and explore complex themes has made him a [13]____________ author among readers of all ages. For undergraduates, studying Steinbeck's works provides an opportunity to delve into the social, historical, and cultural context of the 20th century while [14]____________ the beauty of his prose and the practical significance of his stories.

Listening and Doing

Task ***Scan the QR code to listen to the audio clip "Human Civilization" and decide whether the statements are true (T) or false (F).***

SCAN ME!

1. Paleolithic Age, known as the Old Stone Age, was a remarkable shifting point of human civilization.
2. The appearance of permanent settlements led to the emergence of agriculture.
3. Thanks to work specialization, people could store enough food and establish settled communities.
4. People living in the Neolithic Age could use polished stone tools, pottery, and weaving techniques.
5. People in the Neolithic Age began to create burial sites and monuments to indicate a belief in an afterlife.
6. The progress in agriculture, social structures, technology, and cultural expression in the Stone Ages provides the basis for further development of civilization.

Further Reading

Mini-Pedia — "Amateur" Science Fiction Writers

John Steinbeck, Kurt Vonnegut and Margaret Atwood primarily focused on literary fiction, but they also ventured into writing science fiction.

Kurt Vonnegut (1922-2007) was an American writer known for his unique blend of satire, science fiction, and social commentary. Vonnegut's most famous novel, *Slaughterhouse-Five*, is a darkly humorous and anti-war masterpiece that draws from his own experiences as a prisoner of war during the Allied bombing of Dresden. His other notable works include *Cat's Cradle*, *Breakfast of Champions*, and *Mother Night*.

Vonnegut's writing style was characterized by a mix of black humor, absurdity, and a satirical examination of the human condition. He often explored themes of war, technology, and the dehumanizing effects of modern society. With his sharp wit and distinctive voice, Vonnegut became prominent in American literature, earning both critical acclaim and a devoted readership.

Kurt Vonnegut's works continue to be celebrated for their thought-provoking nature and their ability to challenge societal norms. His contributions to literature have left a lasting impact, solidifying his place as one of the most influential and beloved writers of the 20th century.

Margaret Atwood (1939-) is a renowned Canadian author known for her captivating storytelling and thought-provoking works. Atwood's novels often explore themes of feminism, dystopia, and environmentalism, earning her international acclaim and numerous awards. Her most famous novel, *The Handmaid's Tale*, published in 1985, has become a cultural phenomenon, inspiring a successful television series and sparking important discussions about women's rights and totalitarianism(极权主义).

Aside from her novels, Atwood is also an accomplished poet, essayist, and literary critic. She has published several poetry collections, including *The Circle Game* and *The Door*, showcasing her lyrical prowess and observations of the human condition. Her writing is characterized by its sharp wit, intricate world-building, and compelling characters. Her ability to blend social commentary with compelling narratives has solidified her status as a literary powerhouse.

Throughout her career, Margaret Atwood has left an indelible mark on the literary world, pushing boundaries and challenging readers to examine the complexities of society. Her contributions continue to inspire and resonate with audiences worldwide.

Answer

Unit 3

Isaac Asimov and His Robots (Ⅰ)

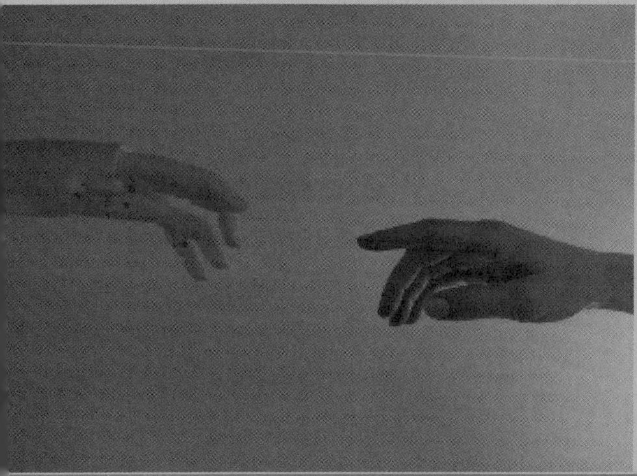

Starting out

Look at the pictures and discuss the following questions.

1. Do you think robots might be dangerous in the future?
2. Will robots replace human beings in the workplace completely?
3. How to deal with the relationship between robots and human beings?
4. Do you think it is possible for a robot to have feelings?
5. If you had a robot, what would you like it to do?

Part 1

Reading and Understanding

I, ROBOT

1 Powell's radio voice was tense in Donovan's ear: "Now, look, let's start with the three *fundamental Rules of Robotics — the three rules that are built most deeply into a robot's **positronic brain**." In the darkness, his gloved fingers ticked off each point.

2 "We have: One, a robot may not injure a human being, or, through inaction, allow a human being to come to harm."

3 "Right!"

4 "Two," continued Powell, "a robot must obey the orders given to it by human beings except where such orders would *conflict with the First Law."

5 "Right!"

6 "And three, a robot must protect its own existence as long as such protection does not conflict with the First or Second Laws."

7 "Right! Now where are we?"

8 "Exactly at the explanation. The conflict between the various rules is *ironed out by the different **positronic potentials** in the brain. We'll say that a robot is walking into danger and knows it. The automatic potential that Rule 3 sets up turns him back. But suppose you order him to walk into that danger. In that case, Rule 2 sets up a **counterpotential** higher than the previous one and the robot follows orders *at the risk of existence."

9 "Well, I know that. What about it?"

10 "Let's take Speedy's case. Speedy is one of the latest models, extremely specialized, and as expensive as a battleship. It's not a thing to be lightly destroyed."

11 "So?"

fundamental 基本的
positronic brain 正子脑
conflict with 和……有冲突
iron out 消除
positronic potential 正子电位
counterpotential 反电位
at the risk of 冒……风险

12 "So Rule 3 has been strengthened — that was specifically mentioned, by the way, in the advance notices on the SPD models — so that his ★**allergy** to danger is unusually high. At the same time, when you sent him out after the **selenium**, you gave him his order ★**casually** and without special emphasis, so that the Rule 2 potential set-up was rather weak. Now, hold on; I'm just stating facts."

13 "All right, go ahead. I think I get it."

14 "You see how it works, don't you? There's some sort of danger centering at the selenium pool. It increases as he ★**approaches**, and at a certain distance from it the Rule 3 potential, unusually high to start with, exactly balances the Rule 2 potential, unusually low to start with."

15 Donovan rose to his feet in excitement. "And it ★**strikes an equilibrium**. I see. Rule 3 drives him back and Rule 2 drives him forward — "

16 "So he follows a circle around the selenium pool, staying on the **locus** of all points of potential equilibrium. And unless we do something about it, he'll stay on that circle forever, giving us the good old runaround." Then, more thoughtfully: "And that, by the way, is what makes him drunk. At potential equilibrium, half the positronic paths of his brain are **out of kilter**. I'm not a robot specialist, but that seems obvious. Probably he's lost control of just those parts of his voluntary mechanism that a human drunk has. Ve-e-ery pretty."

17 "But what's the danger? If we knew what he was running from — "

18 "You suggested it. **Volcanic action**. Somewhere right above the selenium pool is a **seepage** of gas from the bowels of Mercury. Sulphur dioxide, carbon dioxide — and carbon monoxide. Lots of it — and at this temperature."

19 Donovan gulped audibly. "Carbon monoxide plus iron gives

allergy 过敏，反感
selenium 硒
casually 随意地，随便地
approach 接近
strike an equilibrium 达到平衡
locus（某事发生的）确切地点
out of kilter 状态不正常，失灵
volcanic action 火山活动
seepage 渗漏

the volatile iron carbonyl."

20 "And a robot," added Powell, "is essentially iron." Then, grimly: "There's nothing like ★deduction. We've determined everything about our problem but the solution. We can't get the selenium ourselves. It's still too far. We can't send these robot horses, because they can't go themselves, and they can't carry us fast enough to keep us from crisping. And we can't catch Speedy, because the dope thinks we're playing games, and he can run sixty miles to our four."

21 "If one of us goes," began Donovan, ★tentatively, "and comes back cooked, there'll still be the other."

22 "Yes," came the sarcastic reply, "it would be a most tender sacrifice — except that a person would be in no condition to give orders before he ever reached the pool, and I don't think the robots would ever turn back to the cliff without orders. Figure it out! We're two or three miles from the pool — call it two — the robot travels at four miles an hour; and we can last twenty minutes in our suits. It isn't only the heat, remember. Solar ★radiation out here in the ultraviolet and below is poison."

23 "Um-m-m," said Donovan, "ten minutes short."

24 "As good as an eternity. And another thing, in order for Rule 3 potential to have stopped Speedy where it did, there must be an ★appreciable amount of carbon monoxide in the metal-vapor atmosphere — and there must be an appreciable corrosive action therefore. He's been out hours now — and how do we know when a knee joint, for instance, won't be thrown out of kilter and ★keel him over. It's not only a question of thinking — we've got to think fast!"

25 Deep, dark, dank, dismal silence!

26 Donovan broke it, voice trembling in an effort to keep itself emotionless. He said: "As long as we can't increase Rule 2 potential by giving further orders, how about working the other

volatile iron carbonyl 易挥发的羰基铁
deduction 推理，演绎
dope 笨蛋
tentatively 尝试性地
radiation 辐射
ultraviolet 紫外线
eternity 永恒，不朽
appreciable 相当可观的
metal-vapor atmosphere 金属蒸气（构成的）大气
corrosive 腐蚀性的
keel ... over （因疲劳或生病）倒下，瘫倒
dank 阴冷潮湿

way? If we increase the danger, we increase Rule 3 potential and drive him backward."

27 Powell's visiplate had turned toward him in a silent question.

28 "You see," came the cautious explanation, "all we need to do to drive him out of his rut is to increase the concentration of carbon monoxide in his vicinity. Well, back at the Station there's a complete analytical laboratory."

29 "Naturally," assented Powell. "It's a Mining Station."

30 "All right. There must be pounds of oxalic acid for calcium precipitations."

31 "Holy space! Mike, you're a genius."

32 "So-so," admitted Donovan, modestly. "It's just a case of remembering that oxalic acid on heating ★decomposes into carbon dioxide, water, and good old carbon monoxide. College chem, you know."

33 Powell was on his feet and had attracted the attention of one of the monster robots by the simple expedient of pounding the machine's thigh.

34 "Hey," he shouted, "can you throw?"

35 "Master?"

36 "Never mind." Powell damned the robot's molasses-slow brain. He scrabbled up a jagged brick-size rock. "Take this," he said, "and hit the patch of bluish crystals just across the crooked fissure. You see it?"

37 Donovan pulled at his shoulder. "Too far, Greg. It's almost half a mile off."

38 "Quiet," replied Powell. "It's a case of Mercurian gravity and a steel throwing arm. Watch, will you?"

39 The robot's eyes were measuring the distance with machinery accurate stereoscopy. His arm ★adjusted itself to the weight of the missile and drew back. In the darkness, the robot's motions went unseen, but there was a sudden thumping sound as he

visiplate 可视板
rut 一成不变的（模式）
vicinity 周围地区，附近
oxalic acid 草酸
calcium precipitation 钙沉淀
decompose 分解，使腐烂
expedient 权宜之计
molasses-slow brain 迟钝的大脑
fissure（岩石、土地等中深长的）裂缝，裂隙
stereoscopy 立体视觉
adjust ... to 调整，调节

shifted his weight, and seconds later the rock flew blackly into the sunlight. There was no air resistance to slow it down, nor wind to turn it aside — and when it hit the ground it threw up crystals precisely in the center of the "blue patch".

40 Powell yelled happily and shouted, "Let's go back after the oxalic acid, Mike."

41 And as they plunged into the ruined substation on the way back to the tunnels, Donovan said grimly: "Speedy's been hanging about on this side of the selenium pool, ever since we chased after him. Did you see him?"

42 "Yes."

43 "I guess he wants to play games. Well, we'll play him games!"

Developing Ideas

Task 1 Summarize the story and complete the table.

PARAS 1-6	[1] ___________ of Robotics
PARAS 7-16	It's hard for robots to [2] ___________ of potentials because Rule 2 drives robots [3] ___________ while Rule 3 drives them [4] ___________.
PARAS 17-24	The risky situation for robots: ● The [5] ___________ from the center of [6] ___________, especially the [7] ___________ which gives the volatile iron carbonyl with iron. The risky situation for humans to get the selenium: ● They [8] ___________ the selenium themselves, nor [9] ___________.
PARAS 25-43	In order to increase Rule 3 potential, Powell intended to [10] ___________. *Can you guess the solution to the problem?

Task 2 Decide whether the statements are true (T) or false (F) according to the passage.

1. Among the fundamental rules, the first is the most critical one.
2. When a robot identifies a risky area, he will definitely return because of Rule 3.
3. Rule 3 has been strengthened in Speedy's positronic potential, so he was extremely allergic to danger.
4. Speedy follows a circle around the selenium pool because humans give him the order.
5. Powell and Donovan were worried about Speedy in the metal-vapor atmosphere because of corrosive action.
6. Powell threw a jagged brick-size rock and hit the patch of bluish crystal precisely.

Using Language

Task 1 Complete the table with the correct form of the words given. Then complete the sentences with the correct form of the words in the table.

Verb	Noun	Adjective	Adverb
		fundamental	
	allergy		
			casually
approach			
	deduction		
			tentatively
	radiation		
		appreciable	
		corrosive	
decompose			

1. In order to avoid the blindness and ___________ in the tourism products development, it's imperative to study the principles of the design and exploitation.
2. If my ___________ are correct, I can tell you who the killer was.
3. The next round of talks is ___________ scheduled to begin on October 21st in Washington.

4. It contains less than 1 per cent fat, an ____________ amount of protein, and a high content of mineral.
5. They generally agree with the idea that inequality in the information society is ____________ different from that of an industrial society.
6. It's known that tree nuts, such as cashews and walnuts, can trigger serious ____________ reactions.
7. We need to take a more global ____________ to the problem.
8. They discover the link between exposure to ____________ and childhood cancer.
9. Engineers found the structure had been ____________ by moisture.
10. All substances, except those which ____________ when heated, may be changed from one state into another.

Task 2 Complete sentences with the correct form of the phrases in the box.

conflict with	iron out	at the risk of
strike an equilibrium	keel ... over	adjust ... to

1. Their contribution to green technologies can help ____________ between the need for energy and emission reduction.
2. A suppressed immune system puts a transplant recipient ____________ other infections.
3. He held firm opinions which usually ____________ my own, so we were unable to work together.
4. The strong wind made the sailboat ____________ and the passengers fell into the water.
5. Only in this way can the two sides understand each other better and ____________ mutual misunderstanding.
6. There may be a period of disequilibrium as family members ____________ the new baby.

Task 3 Translate the sentences into Chinese.

1. It increases as he approaches, and at a certain distance from it the Rule 3 potential, unusually high to start with, exactly balances the Rule 2 potential, unusually low to start with.

____

____

2. There was no air resistance to slow it down, nor wind to turn it aside — and when it hit the ground it threw up crystals precisely in the center of the "blue patch".

Task 4 Translate the paragraph into English.

在 9 月中国科学家出席的一次会议上发表讲话时，习近平总书记强调了科技创新在中国经济中的战略重要性，并呼吁采取具体措施解决制约技术创新发展的问题。中国可能会将更多资源用于基础研究、前沿研究和技术瓶颈领域，包括芯片和半导体、软件、先进机器人等，更好地保护知识产权，并为研究人员提供更多的市场激励。

Part 2

Appreciating and Comprehending

Robbie

1 Ninety-eight, ninety-nine, one hundred. George, stop bothering Robbie. "But why can't I poke him? Just a little **poke**?" "No!" Gloria *****intervened placatingly**, "He doesn't like it, George. Leave him alone now." The little boy *****subsided**, but his eyes still danced with curiosity and fascination.

2 Robbie stood there as **stolidly** as ever, his face a mask of unalterable good nature. George's poke wouldn't harm a thing, but the positronic brain that held Robbie's **confided personality** could not adequately distinguish between harm and no-harm in this regard. Therefore, he discouraged poking altogether, as he had been doing for the last hour, and would continue to do even after he had won. For a robot is a robot — it can't be anything else but a robot. It can be a thinking, learning, self-correcting robot. It can have the *****semblance** of emotions. It can seem to grow and mature. But it is a robot.

3 Gloria **restored** calmness to the **nursery**, and looked at the two children. George was ten and still an only child and the best playmate he could find was Robbie. She hoped that the coming child would be a little girl. Then things would be easier. She herself had never been afraid of Robbie, but it always *****saddened** her when George's fear reached the point of **loathing**.

4 Robbie had no feelings, no opinions, no knowledge of his own. He **was loaded with** tapes on which were recorded the steps needed to bake a cake or build a house, or play games. When he was given a direction, he merely followed it without any variation. If he seemed to show any *****initiative**, it was purely a simulated show for their benefit, unless the initiative

poke 捅，戳
intervene 打断，插嘴
placatingly 安抚地
subside 消退，趋于平静
stolidly 迟钝地
confided personality 听别人倾诉的性格
semblance 表象，外观
restore 恢复到 (to)
nursery 儿童室
sadden 使伤心，难过
loathe 厌恶，憎恨
be loaded with 装载上
initiative 主动性，积极性

had been ⋆**anticipated** and **allowed for** in his instructions.

5 "Robbie," said Gloria thoughtfully, "do you think George **is** getting too **attached to** you?"

6 Robbie's slow answer came, "What is 'attached,' madam?"

7 Gloria felt **a** sudden **pang of guilt**. Of course, the poor thing wouldn't understand a human emotion.

8 "Never mind, Robbie. You go back to your corner and recharge." Then to George, "You have school tomorrow. It's time for bed."

9 "But I hate school. I don't want to go."

10 "I know, dear. But you have to. Robbie."

11 And the playmate of the youngster for a year **lumbered** to a corner, arms to his sides, stiffly, as though he were some sort of visual statue. Gloria watched him critically; there was something ⋆**disquieting** about the **rigid safety-valve posture**.

12 Gloria thought how every age added something to Robbie's **mechanical body**: it was a child's plaything when new, and prodded and pushed accordingly. It then grew to child's size and its responses slowed so that the little one could **tag its heels**. Larger now, it found it difficult to ⋆**maneuver** in children's **quarters** and became too expensive to be a mere mechanical toy.

13 But it had been designed for children and it was therefore to be a child's ⋆**companion** — and not just a child's toy.

14 Robbie had no consciousness of these gradual **gradations**. He was a machine and, like all machines, a purpose to which he was **ordained**. A robot must obey orders, but give him a set of orders which may lead to a ⋆**contradiction** and he may be ⋆**immobilized**.

15 The positronic brain quivered slightly at the desire to ⋆**disobey** conflicting **sectionals** five years ago, but was immobilized by the **secret professorial code** ⋆**implanted** within it.

anticipate 预见，预料
allow for 考虑到
be attached to 依恋，依附于
a pang of guilt 一阵愧疚
lumber 缓慢吃力地移动
disquieting 令人不安的
rigid safety-valve posture 刻板的疏导情绪的态度
mechanical body 机械身体
tag one's heels 跟在后面
maneuver 灵活操纵
quarter 活动区，住处
companion 同伴
gradation 升级变化
ordain 授予圣职
contradiction 矛盾
immobilize 使不动，停止
disobey 不服从
sectional 组合部分
secret professorial code 秘密专业代码
implant 植入

16Still, Robbie sometimes wondered why he couldn't share such human pleasure as eating, why his cheeks never flushed under any stimulus, why there wasn't an ache or catch in his throat when he missed a note singing. He was filled with **wonder-laced pity** for these poor, incomplete creatures who fleshed his creator.

17Gloria had brought him back from his corner now and George, his schoolbooks under his arm, was staring **glumly** at nothing. She said, "Robbie, show George upstairs."

18Robbie's padded feet made no noise on the thick rugs as he approached from behind and picked up the boy gently but ****unhesitatingly**. George looked over his shoulder, "Hey, his hands are cold."

19 "Hold your schoolbooks correctly," said Gloria sharply. "And say goodbye to Robbie."

20George waved without turning away from the machine. "Goodbye, Robbie."

21 "Goodbye, George."

22Robbie turned back to Gloria. "Madam."

23 "Yes, Robbie?"

24 "Madam, the way George is acting is not good for him."

25 "Why not?"

26 "I apologize, madam, but I cannot answer that question."

27Gloria felt a **vague** disappointment. It would have been nice to be put in her proper place by Robbie's ****conviction** in a matter of child guidance. Perhaps she would get such an answer from her husband.

28Somehow she had never brought up the possibility of Robbie's replacement during her husband's presence. Perhaps it was because she feared the first **fey glimpse into** a supreme complication, a moving toward an automated human factory in which humanity could be lost for the sake of human image.

wonder-laced pity 古怪的怜悯
glumly 闷闷不乐地，阴郁地
unhesitatingly 坚定地，不犹豫地
vague 模糊的
conviction 信念
fey glimpse into 异想天开的短暂感受

29 George's school — for all its *compulsory education, so supposedly necessary for cultural stability — was still a barbarity, since it was a systematized *premature *subordination of life to purpose.

30 Gloria withdrew her mind forcibly from such recent and dangerous thoughts. She wondered if the latter was not her fault, too.

31 Robbie was standing stiffly at attention by her side now. She patted his arm gently thus releasing his control. He trundled motionlessly to his corner and slumped down into a squatting position, his joints unlocked.

32 George lay crossed in his bed, the warm sun coaxing him to sleep. There had been the alarm analogue-shrieking of the automatic teacher right behind him all through the history period and he tried his best to ignore it. He didn't want to think about it.

33 But when the bell rang, he sighed in relief and slouched out of the room.

34 Robbie was standing beside his desk, his blank face staring down and his chest rising and falling artificially in response to the stored air cycles.

35 George growled resentfully, "What are you doing here?"

36 "Waiting for you, George."

37 "So what?"

38 "I wish to speak to you, George. It is important."

compulsory 强制的，义务的
premature 过早的，提前的
subordination 从属于 (to)
stand at attention 立正
trundle 沉重缓慢地走
squat 蹲坐
coax 哄骗
analogue-shrieking 模拟尖叫
slouch 无精打采地做
growl resentfully 不满地咆哮

Developing Ideas

Task Work in groups and discuss the following questions.

1. What's the relationship between George and Robbie?

2. What kind of robot did Robbie look like from the perspective of humanity?
3. What was Gloria worried about?
4. Can you explain Robbie's behavior based on the three fundamental rules?
5. Do you think Robbie was a mere robot?
6. How do you find out Robbie possessed some characteristics of human beings?

Using Language

Task 1 Learn the word formation from the table. Complete the sentences with the correct form of the words in the table.

Word	Prefix	Root	Suffix
intervene	inter- 在……之间，相互	ven 来 + e	/
subside **subordination**	sub- 在……之下	side = sit 坐 ordin 命令	/ +ate 做，造 +tion 名词缀
unhesitatingly	un- 否定前缀	hesitate 犹豫	+ing 形容词缀 +ly 副词缀
disquieting **disobey**	dis- 否定前缀	quiet 使平静 obey 服从	+ing 形容词缀 /
sadden	/	sad 难过的，可悲的	+en 使成为，动词缀
premature	pre- 在……之前	mature	/
immobilize **implant**	im- 否定前缀 im- = in- 使进入某种状态	mobile 可移动的 plant 种植	+ize ……化 /

1. They are required to develop a device to ___________ the car engine in case of theft.
2. Despite the challenge, she ___________ volunteered to lead the rescue mission, demonstrating her unwavering commitment to helping those in need.
3. Fans were ___________ to see the former champion play so badly.
4. It turned out that weak foundations caused the house to ___________.
5. The chairman felt that it was his place to ___________ in the disagreement between two of his committee members.
6. One of the risk factors for ___________ deaths is the air we breathe, over which individuals

have little control.

7. Most confusing and ___________ are the reports of successive failure in investment.
8. The drug is surgically ___________ into a woman's arm where it gradually releases the hormones into the body.

Task 2 Complete the sentences with the correct form of the words in the box.

conviction	compulsory	anticipate	initiative
companion	contradiction	coax	maneuver

1. Chinese authorities have introduced guidelines to ease the burden of excessive homework and off-campus tutoring for students undergoing ___________ education.
2. It makes clear that the principal ___________ facing Chinese society in the new era is that between unbalanced and inadequate development and people's ever-growing needs for a better life.
3. The global race to ___________ more low-carbon tech will be intense in the new year.
4. It is my keenly felt ___________ that an attitude of equality and modesty is required if one wants to truly understand various civilizations.
5. They encouraged employees to use their own ___________ to make decisions without asking managers first.
6. While household robots today do the normal housework, social robots will be much more like ___________ than mere tools.
7. The earlier they learn how computers think, how to ___________ the machine into producing what they want, the better their future will be.
8. Since ancient times, this term has served as a warning to the ruler to govern the country for people, and to ___________ dangers in times of security.

Task 3 Translate the paragraph into Chinese.

Many Chinese companies have launched robotic dogs. For instance, one developed by a tech firm based in Hangzhou, east China's Zhejiang Province, is able to carry a load of 3 kilograms and serve as a running companion for its owner. Last year, electronics manufacturer Xiaomi also unveiled a bipedal humanoid robot that is able to "see" and "sense" its surroundings with face and body recognition technologies. The robot can follow its owner and avoid obstacles automatically.

Thanks to the rising manufacturing capability, robots are no longer exclusive to industrial production.

They are now helping people in many aspects. They are widely employed in domestic service, acting as people's personal assistants, such as robot vacuum and mop, and cooking robot.

(By Peng Xunwen, *People' s Daily,* 2022-10-28)

Part 3

Watching, Listening and Doing

Watching and Doing

SCAN ME!

Task 1 Scan the QR code to watch the video clip "The Life Story of Isaac Asimov (Ⅰ)" and fill in the blanks.

Isaac Asimov, born on January 2, 1920, was an American writer and professor of [1]___________. He wrote and edited more than 500 books and an estimated [2]___________ letters and postcards. He is best known for his works of science [3]___________ and popular science, including the *Foundation* series, the *Robot* series, and the short story *Nightfall*.

Asimov was born in Petrovichi, Russia to Jewish parents; his family moved to the United States when he was three years old. He grew up in Brooklyn, New York, where he [4]___________ public school. He went on to earn a Bachelor of Science in chemistry from Columbia University in 1939 and a PhD in biochemistry from the same university in [5]___________. He worked as a chemist for the Philadelphia Navy Yard during World War Ⅱ.

Asimov began his writing [6]___________ at the age of nineteen, publishing his first story, *Marooned off Vesta*, in *Amazing Stories* in 1939. He went on to become one of the most prolific writers of his time, [7]___________ hundreds of short stories, novels, and non-fiction books throughout his career.

SCAN ME!

Task 2 Scan the QR code to watch the video clip "The Life Story of Isaac Asimov (Ⅱ)" and fill in the blanks.

Asimov is best known for his science fiction works, which helped to [1]___________ the genre in the mid-twentieth century. He is often [2]___________ as one of the "Big Three" science fiction writers of his time, along with Robert A. Heinlein and Arthur C. Clarke.

The *Foundation* series, a series of novels and short stories published between 1942 and 1993, is considered one of Asimov's [3]___________. The series follows the development of psychohistory, a mathematical method for predicting the future, which is used by protagonist Hari Seldon to preserve human knowledge and [4]___________ in the face of an impending collapse of the Galactic Empire. The *Foundation* series won the Hugo Award for Best Series in 1966.

Asimov's *Robot* series, which [5]___________ several novels and short stories published between 1940 and 1985, explores the [6]____________ between humans and intelligent robots, and to what extent robots can be considered to have [7]____________. The series' central character is the robot R. Daneel Olivaw, who appears in several of Asimov's stories.

Asimov also wrote non-fiction books on [8]____________ subjects, including chemistry, mathematics, biology, and history. His popular science books, including *The Intelligent Man's Guide to Science* and *The Human Body: Its Structure and Operation*, helped to explain [9]____________ to the general public.

Throughout his career, Asimov was an outspoken [10]____________ for science and rationalism. He was a [11]____________ to magazines such as *The Magazine of Fantasy & Science Fiction* and *Scientific American*, and wrote a regular column for *Isaac Asimov's Science Fiction Magazine*. In his essays and speeches, he argued that scientific inquiry and rational thought were [12]____________ to solving the world's problems.

Asimov died on April 6, 1992, at the age of 72. His contributions to science fiction and popular science have had a [13]____________ on the genre and on scientific discourse in general. His *Foundation* and *Robot* series have [14]____________ numerous adaptations and continuations, and his non-fiction books remain widely read and influential.

Listening and Doing

Task ***Scan the QR code to listen to the audio clip "Robotics" and decide whether the statements are true (T) or false (F).***

SCAN ME!

☐ 1. As technology develops at a rapid pace, robots are becoming increasingly important.

☐ 2. The purpose of developing robotics is to improve efficiency and reduce human errors.

☐ 3. Some robots with artificial intelligence can learn from experience and improve performance over time.

☐ 4. Some robots can recognize and interpret human language but they can't respond to human emotions.

☐ 5. Robots can help human beings in a wide range of tasks such as healthcare and entertainment.

☐ 6. The potential applications for robotics are becoming increasingly diverse in the future.

Further Reading

Mini-Pedia — American's "Big Three"

Isaac Asimov, Arthur C. Clarke and Robert A. Heinlein are considered as American's "Big Three" western science fiction authors.

Arthur C. Clarke (1917-2008) was a British science fiction writer and futurist, best known for his influential and groundbreaking works in the genre. Some of his most famous works include *2001: A Space Odyssey, Rendezvous with Rama*, and *Childhood's End*. Clarke often explored themes related to the future of humanity, space travel, and advanced technologies in his writing.

In addition to his role as a writer, Clarke was also noted for his scientific and technological contributions. He was a keen inventor and scientist, and a proponent of space exploration, often collaborating with engineers and scientists to develop ideas and designs for space technology. His ideas on the geostationary orbit, a satellite that remained stationary relative to the Earth's surface, led to the development of communication satellite technology.

Clarke's impact on science fiction and popular culture has been significant, and his ideas have been an inspiration for many writers, filmmakers, and scientists. His legacy as a visionary and futurist continues to inspire those interested in science and technology.

Robert A. Heinlein (1907-1988) was a prominent American science fiction writer known for his works in the Golden Age of Science Fiction. Some of his most famous novels include *Stranger in a Strange Land, The Moon Is a Harsh Mistress*, and *Starship Troopers*. Heinlein's writing often explored themes of individualism, freedom, and the complexities of society.

Heinlein was born in Missouri and attended the United States Naval Academy before pursuing a career in writing. His work was often praised for its technical accuracy, scientific rigor, and political commentary. He was also known for his advocacy of space exploration and his contributions to the development of science fiction as a literary genre.

In addition to his writing, Heinlein was also politically active, serving as a member of the California State Assembly and involving himself in numerous political and social causes. He was inducted into the Science Fiction and Fantasy Hall of Fame in 1998, and his legacy as a writer and advocate for science fiction continues to influence the genre to this day.

Answer

Unit 4

Isaac Asimov and His Robots (Ⅱ)

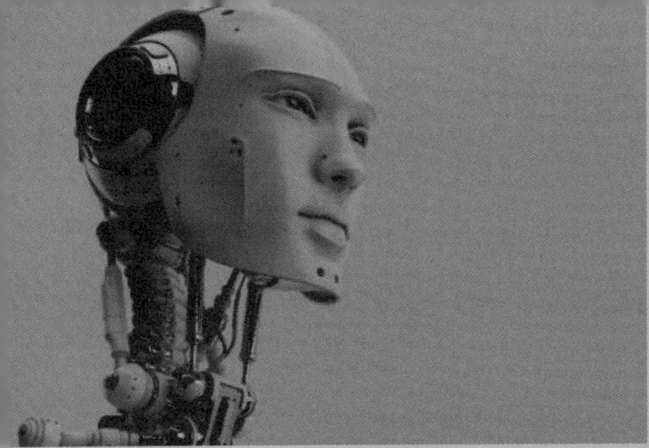

Starting out

Look at the pictures and discuss the following questions.

1. Are robots an accessory to humans?
2. Should robots move around public places as easily as humans?
3. Do robots have the right to be treated with the same respect as humans?
4. Can humans accept the fact that robots will have the same rights as humans?
5. How do we weigh the rights and social status of humans and robots?
6. What kind of law do you think humans would have concerning robots in the future?

Part 1

Reading and Understanding

The Three Laws of Robotics（I）

1 Andrew never quite got to the library.

2 He had studied the map. He knew the route, but not the appearance of it. The actual landmarks did not **resemble** the symbols on the map and he would hesitate.

3 Eventually, he thought he must have somehow gone wrong, for everything looked strange.

4 He passed an ***occasional** field-robot, but by the time he decided he should ask his way none were **in sight**. A vehicle passed and did not stop.

5 Andrew stood **irresolute**, which meant calmly motionless, for coming across the field toward him were two human beings.

6 He turned to face them, and they altered their course to meet him. A moment before, they had been talking loudly. He had heard their voices. But now they were silent. They had the look that Andrew associated with human ***uncertainty**; and they were young, but not very young. Twenty, perhaps? Andrew could never judge human age.

7 "Would you describe to me the route to the town library, sirs?"

8 One of them, the taller of the two, whose tall hat ***lengthened** him still farther, almost **grotesquely**, said, not to Andrew, but to the other, "It's a robot."

9 The other had a **bulbous nose** and heavy eyelids. He said, not to Andrew but to the first, "It's wearing clothes."

10 The tall one **snapped his fingers**. "It's the free robot. They have a robot at the old Martin place who isn't owned by anybody. Why else would it be wearing clothes?"

11 "Ask it," said the one with the nose.

12 "Are you the Martin robot?" asked the tall one.

13 "I am Andrew Martin, sir." Andrew said.

resemble 类似
occasional 临时的
in sight 在视线范围内
irresolute 踌躇不定的
uncertainty 犹豫，无把握
lengthen 使延长，加长
grotesquely 奇异地
bulbous nose 蒜头鼻
snap one's fingers 打响指（表示轻蔑或不在乎）

14 "Good. Take off your clothes. Robots don't wear clothes." He said to the other, "That's disgusting. Look at him!"

15 Andrew hesitated. He hadn't heard an order in that tone of voice in so long that his Second Law circuits had ★**momentarily** jammed.

16 The tall one repeated, "Take off your clothes. I order you."

17 Slowly, Andrew began to remove them.

18 "Just drop them," said the tall one.

19 The nose said, "If it doesn't belong to anyone, it could be ours as much as someone else's."

20 "Anyway," said the tall one, "who's to ★**object to** anything we do. We're not damaging property." He turned to Andrew. "Stand on your head." "The head ★**is** not **meant** — " Andrew began.

21 "That's an order. If you don't know how, try anyway."

22 Andrew hesitated again, then bent to put his head on the ground. He tried to lift his legs but fell, heavily.

23 The tall one said, "Just lie there." He said to the other, "We can take him apart. Ever take a robot apart?"

24 "Will he let us?"

25 "How can he stop us?"

26 There was no way Andrew could stop them, if they ordered him in a ★**forceful** enough manner not to resist. The Second Law of obedience ★**took precedence over** the Third Law of **self-preservation**. In any case, he could not defend himself without possibly hurting them, and that would mean breaking the First Law. At that thought, he felt every **motile** unit **contract** slightly and he quivered as he lay there.

27 The tall one walked over and pushed at him with his foot. "He's heavy. I think we'll need tools to do the job."

28 The nose said, "We could order him to ★**take** himself **apart**. It would be fun to watch him try."

29 "Yes," said the tall one, **thoughtfully**, "but let's get him off the road. If someone comes along —"

momentarily 片刻地
object to 反对
be meant (to do) 理应发生
forceful 强有力的
take precedence over 优先于……
self-preservation 自我保护
motile 能动的
contract 收缩
take apart 拆开
thoughtfully 沉思地

30 It was too late. Someone had, indeed, come along and it was George. From where he lay, Andrew had seen him **topping** a small rise in the middle distance. He would have liked to signal him in some way, but the last order had been "Just lie there!"

31 George was running now, and he arrived on the scene somewhat **winded**. The two young men ⋆**stepped back** a little and then waited thoughtfully.

32 "Andrew, has something gone wrong?" George asked, anxiously.

33 Andrew replied, "I am well, George."

34 "Then stand up. What happened to your clothes?"

35 "That your robot, Mac?" the tall young man asked.

36 George turned sharply. "He's no one's robot. What's been going on here?"

37 "We politely asked him to take his clothes off. What's that to you, if you don't own him."

38 George turned to Andrew. "What were they doing, Andrew?"

39 "It was their intention in some way to **dismember** me. They were about to move me to a quiet spot and order me to dismember myself."

40 George looked at the two young men, and his chin trembled.

41 The young men **retreated** no farther. They were smiling.

42 The tall one said lightly, "What are you going to do, **pudgy**? Attack us?"

43 George said, "No. I don't have to. This robot has been with my family for over seventy-five years. He knows us and he ⋆**values** us more than he values anyone else. I am going to tell him that you two are threatening my life and that you plan to kill me. I will ask him to defend me. In choosing between me and you two, he will choose me. Do you know what will happen to you when he attacks you?"

44 The two were backing away slightly, looking ⋆**uneasy**

45 George said, sharply, "Andrew, I am in danger and about to

top 到达山顶
winded 喘不过气的
step back 后退
dismember 肢解
retreat 后退
pudgy 矮胖的
value 重视，珍视
uneasy 不安的

come to harm from these young men. Move toward them!"

46 Andrew did so, and the young men did not wait. They ran.

47 "All right, Andrew, relax," George said. He looked **unstrung**. He was far past the age where he could face the possibility of a **dustup** with one young man, let alone two.

48 "I couldn't have hurt them, George: I could see they were not attacking you."

49 "I didn't order you to attack them. I only told you to move toward them. Their own fears did the rest."

50 "How can they fear robots?"

51 "It's a disease of mankind, one which has not yet been cured. But never mind that. **What the devil** are you doing here, Andrew? Good thing I found your note. I was just on the point of turning back and hiring a helicopter when I found you. How did you get it into your **head to** go to the library? I would have brought you any books you needed."

52 "I am a — " Andrew began.

53 "Free robot. Yes, yes. All right, what did you want in the library?"

54 "I want to know more about human beings, about the world, about everything. And about robots, George. I want to write a history about robots."

55 George put his arm on the other's shoulder. "Well, let's walk home. But pick up your clothes first. Andrew, there are a million books on robotics and all of them include histories of the science. The world ⋆**is** growing **saturated** not only **with** robots but with information about robots."

56 Andrew shook his head, a human gesture he had lately begun to ⋆**adopt**. "Not a history of robotics, George. A history of robots, by a robot. I want to explain how robots feel about what has happened since the first ones were allowed to work and live on Earth."

57 George's eyebrows lifted, but he said nothing in direct response.

unstrung 焦虑不安的
dustup 争吵，吵闹
what the devil (用于强调) 究竟，到底
head to 前往
be saturated with 充满着
adopt 采用，采取

Developing Ideas

Task 1 Summarize the story and complete the table.

PARAS 1-4	Andrew, a [1]____________ robot, wanted to [2]____________, but he was lost on his way.
PARAS 5-29	Two young men were unfriendly to Andrew and they ordered him to: ● [3]____________ his clothes; ● [4]____________ his head; ● [5]____________ on the ground; ● [6]____________ himself. There is no way Andrew could stop them, because [7]____________ took precedence over [8]____________ in spite of the fact that: ● His Second Law circuits [9]____________; ● He felt [10]____________ slightly and he quivered as he lay there.
PARAS 30-49	George had an intimate relationship with Andrew and saved him in time by taking the advantage of the Rules. The young men's responses such as: ● [11]____________ and waiting thoughtfully, ● [12]____________ and smiling, ● backing away slightly and [13]____________, ● [14]____________ without waiting, showed the changes in their attitude and their [15]____________.
PARAS 50-57	Andrew told George he was going to the library in order to become the first robot writer [16]____________. *Can Andrew achieve his dream? Will the situation of robots be changed in the future?

Task 2 Decide whether the statements are true (T) or false (F) according to the passage.

☐ 1. Andrew didn't meet any other robots on his way to the library.

☐ 2. Andrew is the robot owned only by old Martin.

3. Andrew had no way of protecting himself from being torn apart.

4. Andrew couldn't protect George when he was in danger.

5. Two young men run away because they were afraid to hurt George.

6. Andrew wanted to write a book about the history of robots.

Using Language

Task 1 Complete the table with the correct form of the words given. Then complete the sentences with the correct form of the words in the table.

Verb	Noun	Adjective	Adverb
		forceful	
		occasional	
	uncertainty		
lengthen			
value			
adopt			
		uneasy	
			momentarily

1. They planned to take the enemy position by strategy instead of by ____________ attack.
2. After the peace talk, the two sides eventually reached a ____________ compromise.
3. The photographers managed to capture Jane, one of the most famous actresses, on an unguarded ____________.
4. As nights were ____________ with the coming of winter, they had to store enough coal for heating.
5. The ____________ created by this situation must be confusing for you.
6. While their parents were content to work long hours, young people ____________ flexibility.
7. The method with less costs and higher economic benefits is certainly ____________ in the production.
8. The King was silent and thoughtful for a while, and his face betrayed a growing distress and ____________.

Task 2 Complete the sentences with the correct form of the phrases in the box.

take precedence over	object to	be saturated with
step back	take apart	be meant to do

1. Business people think that fluency and communication ___________ grammar when speaking.
2. When the radio DJ who ___________ host the program failed to turn up, the studio manager asked her to stand in.
3. We are learning to ___________ from ourselves and identify our strengths and weaknesses.
4. Anything that's simple can't be destroyed for it has no parts to ___________.
5. The whole conversation ___________ tension and depression due to the sudden arrival of the unexpected visitor.
6. He ___________ expressing his inner views in public because of harsh criticism from the outside media.

Task 3 Translate the sentences into Chinese.

1. There was no way Andrew could stop them, if they ordered him in a forceful enough manner not to resist. The Second Law of obedience took precedence over the Third Law of self-preservation.

____

____

2. This robot has been with my family for over seventy-five years. He knows us and he values us more than he values anyone else. I am going to tell him that you two are threatening my life and that you plan to kill me. I will ask him to defend me.

____

____

____

____

Task 4 Translate the paragraph into English.

ChatGPT 是 OpenAI 开发的先进语言模型，代表了自然语言处理技术的重大突破。ChatGPT 能够理解和处理人类语言输入，使用户能够以对话的方式与模型互动。它理解语境、细微差别和用户提示，提供相关连贯的回答。该模型广泛的训练数据使其能够讨论各种主题，从常识性知识到专业领域。它可以协助用户回答问题、提供解释，并在各个领域进行讨论。ChatGPT 可以为各种用途生成文本内容，如撰写文章、报告、电子邮件或创意作品。它可以帮助用户高效地起草文本，并为内容创作提供创意。尽管它展示了出色的能力，但用户应该了解其局限性和潜在的偏见，以明智和批判性的方式使用它。

Appreciating and Comprehending

The Three Laws of Robotics (Ⅱ)

1 Little Miss was just past her eighty-third birthday, but there was nothing about her that **was lacking in** either energy or determination. She gestured with her **cane** oftener than she **propped herself up** with it.

2 She listened to the story *__in a fury of indignation__. "George, that's horrible. Who were those young **ruffians**?"

3 "I don't know. What difference does it make? In the end they did not do any damage."

4 "They might have. You're a lawyer, George; and if you're **well off**, it's entirely due to the talents of Andrew. It was the money he earned that is the foundation of everything we have. He provides the continuity for this family, and I will not have him treated as a **wind-up** toy."

5 "What would you have me do, Mother?" George asked.

6 "I said you're a lawyer. Don't you listen? You set up a test case somehow, and you force the regional courts to **declare for** robot rights and get the **legislature** to pass the necessary bills. Carry the whole thing to the World Court, if you have to. I'll be watching, George, and I'll **tolerate** no shirking."

7 She was serious, so what began as a way of **soothing** the *__fearsome__ old lady became an **involved** matter with enough legal *__entanglement__ to make it interesting. As senior partner of Feingold and Martin, George **plotted** strategy. But he left the actual work to his junior partners, with much of it a matter for his son, Paul, who was also a member of the firm and who reported **dutifully** nearly every day to his grandmother.

8 She, in turn, discussed the case every day with Andrew.

9 Andrew was deeply *__involved__. His work on his book on

be lacking in 缺乏
cane 拐杖
prop oneself up 支撑
in a fury of indignation 勃然大怒
ruffian 无赖
well off 富裕的
wind-up 装有发条的
declare for 表态支持
legislature 立法机关
tolerate 容许
soothe 安慰
fearsome 可怕的
involved 复杂的
entanglement 纠缠
plot 制订
dutifully 忠实地
involved 专心的；参与的

robots was delayed again, as he *pored over the legal arguments and even, at times, made very *diffident suggestions.

10 "George told me that day I was attacked that human beings have always been afraid of robots," he said one day. "As long as they are, the courts and the legislatures are not likely to work hard on behalf of robots. Should not something be done about public opinion?"

11 So while Paul stayed in court, George took to the public platform. It gave him the advantage of being informal, and he even went so far sometimes as to wear the new, loose style of clothing which he called drapery.

12 Paul chided him, "Just don't *trip over it on stage, Dad."

13 George replied, despondently, "I'll try not to."

14 He addressed the annual convention of holo-news editors on one occasion and said, *in part: "If, *by virtue of the Second Law, we can demand of any robot unlimited obedience in all respects not involving harm to a human being, then any human being, any human being, has a fearsome power over any robot, any robot. In particular, since Second Law *supersedes Third Law, any human being can use the law of obedience to overcome the law of self-protection. He can order any robot to damage itself or even to destroy itself for any reason, or for no reason.

15 "Is this just? Would we treat an animal so? Even an *inanimate object which had given us good service has a claim on our consideration. And a robot is not *insensitive; it is not an animal. It can think well enough so that it can talk to us, *reason with us, joke with us. Can we treat them as friends; can we work together with them, and not give them some of the fruits of that friendship, some of the benefits of co-working?

16 "If a man has the right to give a robot any order that does not involve harm to a human being, he should have the decency never to give a robot any order that involves harm to a robot,

pore over 仔细阅读
diffident 谦虚谨慎的
drapery 窗帘
chide 责骂
trip over 绊倒
despondently 沮丧地
address 发表演说
convention 会议
holo-news 全息新闻
in part 部分地
by virtue of 凭借，由于
supersede 替代，取代
inanimate 无生命的
insensitive 感觉迟钝的
reason with sb. 和……讲道理
decency 体面

unless human safety absolutely requires it. With great power goes great responsibility, and if the robots have Three Laws to protect men, is it too much to ask that men have a law or two to protect robots?"

17 Andrew was right. It was the battle over public opinion that held the key to courts and legislature. In the end, a law was passed that set up conditions under which robot-harming orders were forbidden. It was **endlessly** qualified and the punishments for violating the law were totally **inadequate**, but the principle was established. The final passage by the World Legislature came through on the day of Little Miss' death.

18 That was no **coincidence**. Little Miss ★**held on to** life **desperately** during the last debate and let go only when word of victory arrived. Her last smile was for Andrew.

19 Her last words were, "You have been good to us, Andrew." She died with her hand holding his, while her son and his wife and children remained at a **respectful** distance from both.

endlessly 永久地
inadequate 不充分的
coincidence 巧合
hold on to 坚持，紧握
desperately 不顾一切地
respectful 表示敬意的

Developing Ideas

Task Work in groups and discuss the following questions.

1. Why was Little Miss so angry?
2. What was the implication of the request of Little Miss to ask George to push for the bill?
3. What did Andrew think was the key to the legislature's passage?
4. Why did society need laws to protect robots?
5. What was the result of the law that was finally enacted?

Using Language

Task 1 Learn the word formation from the table. Complete the sentences with the correct form of the words in the table.

Word	Prefix	Root	Suffix
indignation **inanimate** **insensitive**	in- 不，非，相反的	dign 高贵 anim 生命 sens 感觉	+ation 名词缀 +ate 具有……的 +itive 形容词缀
entanglement	en-(=make) 使	tangle 纠结	+ment 名词缀
diffident	di- 否定前缀	fid 相信	+ent 形容词缀
illuminated	il- 使……进入	lumin 光	+ate 做，造成
fearsome	/	fear 害怕	+some 表形容词，充满……的，具有……倾向的
supersede	super- 在上，上方	sed, 坐，词源同“sit”	/
involved	in- 内部，包含	volv 内部，包含	+ed 形容词缀

1. They usually have quite different opinions, but it is a mere ____________ that they see eye to eye on this point.
2. With the outbreak of the first Industrial Revolution, the shift it brought about has seen the use of machines ____________ manual labor.
3. For years after her husband's death, she kept herself to herself, avoiding emotional ____________ with other people.
4. It is reported that the rise in train fares has aroused public ____________.
5. He wondered if ____________ objects might have a mental existence.
6. If we do not improve the awareness of environmental safety protection, the negative impact on the earth and human beings in the future is very ____________.
7. Local residents are ____________ to the new garbage sorting policy because of the complexity of the operation.
8. The official was ____________ in a civil dispute because of a complaint from a local resident.

Task 2 Complete the sentences with the correct form of the phrases in the box.

in part	reason with	pore over
by virtue of	hold on to	trip over

1. ___________ her innate physical advantages and the efforts of the day after tomorrow, she achieved the first place in the competition.
2. It will be a great pleasure to listen to some soft music, ___________ several pages of a good book and have a nice sleep at your leisure time.
3. I have watched parents trying to ___________ their children and have never seen it work.
4. In her acceptance speech, she modestly mentioned that her success was due ___________ to good luck.
5. No matter what difficulties she encountered, she would always ___________ the agreement she promised her mother.
6. You'd better remove the bike from the road because someone might ___________ it.

Task 3 Translate the paragraph into Chinese.

Chinese home appliance manufacturers are stepping up efforts to integrate AI-powered chatbots into their products and services. They hope to provide a better human-machine interaction experience, as ChatGPT has triggered worldwide attention and a new AI wave due to its advanced conversational capabilities.

Home appliance maker Midea Group is among the first batch of partners for Ernie Bot, a ChatGPT-like AI chatbot launched by technology heavyweight Baidu in March. Midea said it would bolster the upgrading of human-machine conversation abilities in the smart home sector by using cutting-edge generative AI technology.

(By Fan Feifei, *China Daily,* 2023-06-29)

Part 3

Watching, Listening and Doing

Watching and Doing

SCAN ME!

Task 1 Scan the QR code to watch the video clip "The Bicentennial Man (Ⅰ)" and fill in the blanks.

The Bicentennial Man (双百人) is a [1]____________ science fiction novel by American science fiction writer Isaac Asimov. This novel was first published in [2]____________ and is one of Asimov's most famous works.

The Bicentennial Man is a work that combines elements of science fiction, [3]____________, and sociology. The story of the novel takes place on the future Earth, and human society has [4]____________ into a highly mechanized and automated stage. In order to solve the problem of [5]____________, residents on Earth are limited to living in a closed environment called "cities". These cities are [6]____________ of countless huge buildings, and people live in highly planned and controlled environments.

The protagonist of the story is a [7]____________ named Andrew Harding. He is very interested in the past human society, especially regarding issues of human [8]____________ and individual consciousness. In his research, he discovered a [9]____________ phenomenon where people in cities began to exhibit abnormal behavior and thinking. They began to show a desire for freedom and [10]____________ with the control system in the city.

SCAN ME!

Task 2 Scan the QR code to watch the video clip "The Bicentennial Man (Ⅱ)" and fill in the blanks.

Harding decided to [1]____________ an investigation, hoping to find the reasons behind these [2]____________ behaviors. In his research, he met a robot psychologist named Donovan. Donovan is a very intelligent and [3]____________ thinking robot, and he has become an important partner of Harding.

Through their [4]____________, Harding and Donovan gradually revealed the secrets in the city. They found a flaw in the city's control system that [5]____________ people's thinking and behavior. And this defect is caused by an error in the city's [6]____________.

In order to solve this problem, Harding and Donovan decided to confront the city's control system and attempted to [7]___________ people's sense of freedom. They face enormous difficulties and risks, but they firmly believe in the importance of freedom and individual consciousness, and are [8]___________ to strive for it.

The novel *The Bicentennial Man* raises a series of profound questions through its vision of the future society and [9]___________ of the human mind. It explores the relationship between technology and human freedom, as well as the importance of individual consciousness in society. Asimov's story has a [10]___________ and captivating plot, while also providing readers with thoughts and inspiration for the future of [11]___________. It not only showcases Asimov's talent as a great science fiction writer, but also brings people to think about future society and human freedom.

Listening and Doing

Task ***Scan the QR code to listen to the audio clip "Self-replicating Robots" and decide whether the statements are true (T) or false (F).***

SCAN ME!

1. Since self-replicating machines made in the United States are extremely simple, they perform no functions.
2. It is possible to design and produce robots that can reproduce, repair themselves or even assemble components into completely new machines.
3. Robots with the ability to construct replicas often bring about disastrous consequences for humanity.
4. The first self-reproducing robot replicated itself by picking up new cubes and assembling them into a new functional machine.
5. It has been shown, with reliable experimental support, that mechanical self-reproduction is possible and unique to biology.
6. The replica constructed by the four-module robot is smaller than the original.

Further Reading

Mini-Pedia — Authors Known for Their Series

Frank Herbert, a famous American science fiction writer, was born in 1920 and died in 1986. He is best known for his *Dune* series.

In the *Dune* series, Herbert creates a future world filled with political struggles, power struggles, and religious beliefs. Through the experiences of his protagonist Paul Atred, he shows the conflicts and challenges of a desolate planet ruled by sand dunes. The series is widely considered a classic of science fiction literature and has had a profound influence on subsequent works.

In addition to the *Dune* series, Herbert also wrote many other well-known works, His works are not only successful in the science fiction literature circle, but also deeply loved by the majority of readers. Herbert, with his unique style and depth of thought, has become one of the important figures in science fiction literature circle.

C. J. Cherryh, whose full name is Carolyn Janice Cherry, was born on September 1, 1942, and has authored numerous novels that have garnered critical acclaim and a dedicated fan base.

One of Cherryh's most notable achievements is her creation of the *Foreigner* series, which focuses on the interactions between humans and an alien species known as the atevi. This series delves into themes of diplomacy, cultural clashes, and the challenges of understanding and coexisting with beings of different backgrounds.

Throughout her career, Cherryh has received numerous accolades, including the prestigious Hugo Award and the John W. Campbell Award for Best New Writer. Her impact on the science fiction and fantasy genres is profound, and her ability to blend intricate storytelling with sociopolitical exploration has solidified her place as a literary force in speculative fiction.

Answer

Unit 5

Katherine Maclean and Her Women Sci-Fi

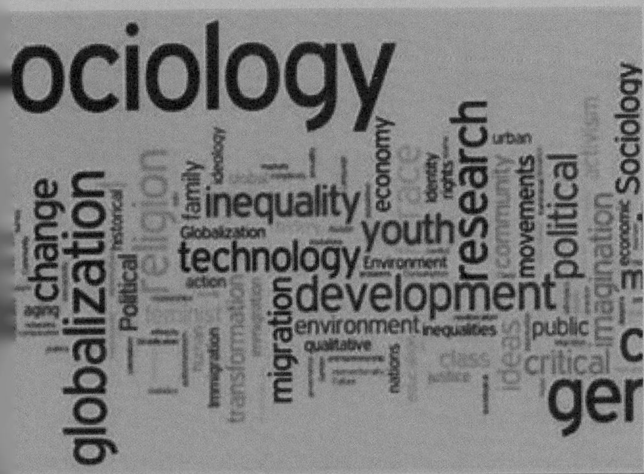

Starting out

Look at the pictures and discuss the following questions.

1. How much do you know about sociology?
2. Have you ever heard of the snowball effect?
3. Do you think sociology is useful in our daily life? Give an example.
4. When more and more people around you join an organization, will you follow the crowd and become part of it?
5. Before an experiment, do you think the subjects should know the details of the experiment?
6. How do we ensure that social experimentation is ethical and safe?

Part 1

Reading and Understanding

The Snowball Effect (Ⅰ)

1 "That's theory," I said. "How about proof?"

2 "My **equations** are already being used in the study of limited-size Federal corporations. Washington — "

3 I held up my palm again. "Please, not that **nasty** word again. I mean, where else has it been ***put into operation**? Just a simple demonstration, something to show that it works, that' s all."

4 He looked away from me thoughtfully, picked up the book and began to tap it on the desk again. It had some unreadable title and his name on it in gold letters. I got the distinct impression again that he was ***repressing** an urge to hit me with it.

5 He spoke quietly. "All right. I'll give you a demonstration. Are you willing to wait six months?"

6 "Certainly, if you can show me something at the end of that time."

7 **Reminded of** time, I glanced at my watch and stood up.

8 "Could we discuss this over lunch?" he asked.

9 "I wouldn't mind hearing more, but I'm having lunch with some **executors** of a millionaire's will. They have to be convinced that by "**furtherance** of research into human ills" he meant that the money should go to research **fellowships** for postgraduate biologists at the university, rather than to a medical foundation."

10 "I see you have your problems, too," Caswell said, **conceding** me nothing. He extended his hand with a chilly smile. "Well, good afternoon, Mr. Halloway. I'm glad we had this talk."

11 I shook hands and left him standing there, sure of his place in the progress of science and the respect of his colleagues, yet

equation 等式，方程式
nasty 令人不快的
put into operation 生效
repress 压抑
remind ... of 提醒
executor 执行人
furtherance 促进
fellowship 奖学金
concede 承认

seething inside because I, the president and dean, had **boorishly** demanded that he produce something **tangible**.

12 My job isn't easy. For a **crumb** of favourable publicity and respect in the newspapers and an annual ceremony in a silly costume, I spend the rest of the year ***going hat in hand**, asking politely for money at everyone's door, like a well-dressed **panhandler**, and trying to manage the university on the **dribble** I get. As far as I was concerned, a department had to support itself or be ***cut down** to what student tuition pays for, which is a handful of overcrowded courses taught by an assistant lecturer. Caswell had to make it work or get out.

13 But the more I thought about it, the more I wanted to hear what he was going to do for a demonstration.

14 At lunch, three days later, while we were waiting for our order, he opened a small notebook. "Ever hear of feedback effects?"

15 "Not enough to have it clear."

16 "You know the snowball effect though."

17 "Sure, start a snowball rolling downhill and it grows."

18 "Well, now — " He wrote a short line of symbols on a blank page and turned the notebook around for me to ***inspect** it. "Here's the **formula** for the snowball process. It's the basic general growth formula — covers everything."

19 It was a row of little symbols arranged like an ***algebra** equation. One was a **concentric spiral** going up, like a **cross-section** of a snowball rolling in snow. That was a growth sign.

20 I hadn't expected to understand the equation, but it was almost as clear as a sentence. I was impressed and slightly ***intimidated** by it. He had already explained enough so that I knew that, if he was right, here was the growth of the Catholic Church and the Roman Empire, the conquests of Alexander and

seethe 生闷气
boorishly 粗鲁无礼地
tangible 有形的
crumb 少量
go hat in hand 低三下四地乞求
panhandler 乞丐
dribble 少量的钱
cut down 削减开支
inspect 检查
formula 公式
algebra 代数学
concentric 同中心的
spiral 螺线
cross-section 横截面
intimidate 威吓

the spread of the smoking habit and the change and *rigidity of the unwritten law of styles.

21 "Is it really as simple as that?" I asked.

22 "You notice," he said, "that when it becomes too heavy for the cohesion strength of snow, it breaks apart. Now in human terms — "

23 The chops and mashed potatoes and peas arrived.

24 "Go on," I urged.

25 He was deep in the symbology of human motives and the equations of human behaviour in groups. After *running through a few different types of grower and shrinker type organizations, we came back to the snowball, and decided to run the test by making something grow.

26 "You add the motives," he said, "and the equation will translate them into organization."

27 "How about a good selfish reason for the ins to drag others into the group — some sort of bounty on new members, a cut of their membership fee?" I suggested uncertainly, feeling slightly foolish. "And maybe a reason why the members would lose if any of them resigned, and some indirect way they could use to force each other to stay in."

28 "The first is the chain letter principle," he nodded. "I've got that. The other …" He put the symbols through some mathematical *manipulation so that a special grouping appeared in the middle of the equation. "That's it."

29 Since I seemed to have the right idea, I suggested some more, and he added some, and juggled them around in different patterns. We threw out a few that would have made the organization too complicated, and finally worked out an *idyllically simple and deadly little organization set-up where joining had all the temptation of buying a sweepstakes ticket, going in deeper was as easy as hanging around a race track, and

rigidity 僵化
cohesion 内聚力
chop（猪、羊）排
symbology 符号学
run through 匆匆浏览
translate 转变
bounty 赏金，奖金
chain letter 连环信
manipulation 运算
juggle 兼顾
idyllically 质朴宜人地
sweepstake 赌金独得制

getting out was like trying to pull free from a Malayan thumb trap. We put our heads closer together and talked lower, picking the best place for the demonstration.

30 "Abington?"

31 "How about Watashaw? I have some student sociological surveys of it already. We can pick a suitable group from that."

32 "This demonstration has got to be *convincing. We'd better pick a little group that no one in his right mind would expect to grow."

33 "There should be a suitable club — "

34 "Ladies," said the skinny female chairman of the Watashaw Sewing Circle. "Today we have guests." She signaled for us to rise, and we stood up, bowing to polite applause and smiles. "Professor Caswell, and Professor Smith" (My alias.) "They are making a survey of the methods and duties of the clubs of Watashaw."

35 We sat down to another ripple of applause and slightly wider smiles, and then the meeting of the Watashaw Sewing Circle began. In five minutes, I began to feel sleepy.

36 There were only about thirty people there, and it was a small room, not the halls of Congress, but they discussed their business of collecting and repairing second-hand clothing for charity with the same endless boring parliamentary formality.

37 I pointed out to Caswell the member I thought would be the natural leader, a tall, well-built woman in a green suit, with conscious gestures and a resonant, penetrating voice, and then went into a half doze while Caswell stayed awake beside me and wrote in his notebook. After a while the resonant voice roused me to attention for a moment. It was the tall woman holding the floor over some collective dereliction of the club. She was being scathing.

38 I nudged Caswell and murmured, "Did you fix it so that a

convincing 有说服力的
in one's right mind 神志清醒
skinny 皮包骨的
alias 别名，化名

shover has a better chance of getting into office than a non-shover?"

39 "I think there's a way they could find for it," Caswell whispered back, and went to work on his equation again. "Yes, several ways to bias the elections."

40 "Good. Point them out tactfully to the one you select. Not as if she'd use such methods, but just as an example of the reason why only she can be trusted with initiating the change. Just mention all the personal advantages an unscrupulous person could have."

41 He nodded, keeping a straight and sober face as if we were exchanging admiring remarks about the techniques of clothes repairing, instead of conspiring.

42 After the meeting, Caswell drew the tall woman in the green suit aside and spoke to her confidentially, showing her the diagram of organization we had drawn up. I saw the responsive glitter in the woman's eyes and knew she was hooked.

43 We left the diagram of organization and our typed copy of the new by-laws with her and went off soberly, as befitted two social science experimenters. We didn't start laughing until our car passed the town limits and began the climb for University Heights.

44 If Caswell's equations meant anything at all, we had given that sewing circle more growth drives than the Roman Empire.

Developing Ideas

Task 1 Summarize the story and complete the table.

PARAS 1-13	Mr. Halloway was initially doubtful about Caswell's equations in sociology and asked him to give a simple [1]____________ Caswell agreed to show it [2]____________. ● Mr. Halloway was [3]____________ of the university and tried to [4]____________. ● Caswell was the professor who attained his place [5]____________ and [6]____________ of his colleagues.
PARAS 14-29	Caswell explained the snowball effect to Mr. Halloway three days later. ● The Snowball effect means a snowball will grow when it starts to [7]____________. ● The growth formula for the snowball process is the [8]____________ one that [9]____________. ● When the snowball becomes [10]____________ of snow, it breaks apart. Mr. Halloway and Caswell decided to [11]____________ by making something grow. ● They discussed and refined their ideas, finally working out an [12]____________ plan. ● The organization set-up would encourage people to [13]____________ and make it difficult for them to [14]____________. They chose [15]____________ in Watashaw and started the demonstration.
PARAS 30-44	● They chose a member to be the natural leader and gave her the [16]____________ to help with the growth of the club. ● The comparison to the [17]____________ suggests that the sewing circle's growth may reach a historically significant level. *Can you predict the growth track of the club?

Task 2 Decide whether the statements are true (T) or false (F) according to the passage.

☐ 1. Sociological studies have never been applied to policy-making area by authorities in Washington.

☐ 2. Catwell hit the president on the head with a book when the president couldn't believe the effectiveness of his equation.

☐ 3. The president and dean had to cater to people in different fields in order to raise money for the management of the university.

☐ 4. The university was quite popular and a handful of courses were overcrowded.

☐ 5. The equation of the snowball process is likely to explain the growth of Catholic Church as well as the spread of smoking habit.

☐ 6. The tall woman in the green suit was chosen as the leader because she was the only one that could be trusted by two professors.

☐ 7. The professors were delighted on their way back to the university because their survey of the methods and duties of the clubs went smoothly.

Using Language

Task 1 Complete the table with the correct form of the words given. Then complete the sentences with the correct form of the words in the table.

Verb	Noun	Adjective	Adverb
repress			
		convincing	
	cohesion		
concede			
			confidentially
	intimidate		
	algebra		
			idyllically
		resonant	
initiate			

1. The heartfelt speech delivered by the speaker struck a chord with the audience, creating a ___________ of shared emotions and inspiring a collective call for change.
2. The society's ___________ attitudes towards women in the workforce hindered the open expression of their desires and preferences.
3. The mathematician used advanced ___________ equations to solve the complex problem.
4. He pressed the button to ___________ the launch sequence, starting the countdown for the rocket's liftoff.
5. The beautiful beach with its crystal-clear waters created an ___________ setting for a relaxing vacation.
6. The presence of the towering security guards at the entrance served as a clear ___________ tactic, discouraging anyone from causing trouble at the event.
7. Peter has a strong record of success, which makes him highly ___________ in his ability to complete the new project.
8. The members of the group remained remarkably ___________ and they could defeat any competitors.
9. After losing this decisive battle, the general was forced to ___________, which ultimately ended the war.
10. The company's financial statements are highly ___________ and should only be accessed by authorized personnel.

Task 2 Complete the sentences with the correct form of the words and phrases in the box.

go hat in hand	cut down	inspect	tangible
put into operation	run through	manipulate	rigidity

1. In an effort to reduce costs and promote sustainability, the company decided to ___________ on paper usage by implementing digital document management systems.
2. Despite his initial reluctance, he had no choice but to ___________ to ask his parents for financial assistance during his time of need.
3. After months of planning and preparation, the new manufacturing facility was finally ___________, marking a significant milestone for the company's expansion.
4. The security diligently ___________ every corner of the building to ensure that it met all safety

regulations and standards.

5. The artist's sculptures were admired for their intricate details and realistic forms, making the intangible concept of emotions ___________ through art.
6. I decided to quickly ___________ my presentation one more time to ensure that I had covered all the key points before the meeting.
7. It is unethical to ___________ others for personal gain or to deceive them for one's own benefit.
8. The ___________ of his mindset prevented him from considering alternative perspectives or adapting to new ideas, making him resistant to change.

Task 3 Translate the sentences into Chinese.

1. My job isn't easy. For a crumb of favourable publicity and respect in the newspapers and an annual ceremony in a silly costume, I spend the rest of the year going hat in hand, asking politely for money at everyone's door, like a well-dressed panhandler, and trying to manage the university on the dribble I get.

____

____

____

____

2. I hadn't expected to understand the equation, but it was almost as clear as a sentence. I was impressed and slightly intimidated by it. He had already explained enough so that I knew that, if he was right, here was the growth of the Catholic Church and the Roman Empire, the conquests of Alexander and the spread of the smoking habit and the change and rigidity of the unwritten law of styles.

____

____

____

____

Task 4 Translate the paragraph into English.

中国的试点治理(pilot governance)概念可以追溯到公元前 169 年,并体现在不同时期的国家治理实践中。改革开放以来,中央政府广泛采用试点治理。特别是经济特区(SEZs)、经济技术开发区(ETDZs)和高新技术产业开发区(HIDZs)已成为中国区域经济改革和发展的重要试验田。试点治理是一个循序渐进的改革过程,它鼓励地方政府和个人自主进行改革探索和试验。试点治理使中央政府能够从地方改革先行者的自下而上实验中积累经验,这些经验可以作为自上而下的试点政策在更多或全部地区实施。直到现在,"试点"一词经常出现在中国的官方文件中,试点治理已成为中国改革和政策的流行范式(paradigm)。

Part 2

Appreciating and Comprehending

The Snowball Effect（Ⅱ）

1 The first day of the sixth month, a big two-page **spread** appeared in the local paper of a **mass meeting** which had approved a **full-fledged** scheme for **slum clearance** of Watashaw's **shack-town** section, plus plans for rehousing, **civic** building, and re-zoning. And good ★**prospects** for attracting some new industries to the town, industries which had already been contacted and seemed interested by the ★**privileges** offered.

2 And with all this, an arrangement for securing and distributing to the club members alone most of the profit that would come to the town in the form of a rise in the price of building sites and a boom in the building industry. The profit distributing arrangement was the same one that had been built into the organization plan for the distribution of the small profits of membership fees and honorary promotions. It was becoming an openly profitable business. Membership was rising more rapidly now.

3 By the second week of the sixth month, news appeared in the local paper that the club had ★**filed an application** to ★**incorporate** itself as the Watashaw Mutual Trade and Civic Development Corporation, and all the local **real estate** promoters had finished joining **en masse**. The **Mutual** Trade part sounded to me as if the Chamber of Commerce was on the point of being pulled in with them, ideas, ambitions, and all.

4 I **chuckled** while reading the next page of the paper, on which a local politician was reported as having addressed the club with a long flowery **oration** on their enterprise, charity, and civic spirit. He had been made an honorary member. If he

spread（书籍、杂志、报纸中）横贯两版的篇幅
mass meeting 群众大会
full-fledged 完备的
slum clearance 贫民窟拆迁
shack-town 贫民区
civic 市民的
prospect 希望
privilege 特权
file an application 提出申请
incorporate 合并
real estate 房地产
en masse 全体
mutual 相互的
chuckle 轻声地笑笑
oration 演讲

allowed himself to be made a ⋆**full member** with its **contractual obligations** and its **lures**, if the politicians went into this, too ...

5 I laughed, filing the newspaper with the other documents on the Watashaw test. These proofs would fascinate any businessman with the sense to see where his bread was buttered. A businessman is constantly dealing with organizations, including his own, and finding them either **inert**, **cantankerous**, or both. Caswell's formula could be a handle to grasp them with. Gratitude alone would bring money into the university in **car-load** lots.

6 The end of the sixth month came. The test was over and the end reports were spectacular. Caswell's formulas were proven ⋆**to the hilt**.

After reading the last newspaper reports, I called him up.

7 "Perfect, Wilt, ⋆perfect! I can use this Watashaw thing to get you so many fellowships and scholarships and **grants** for your department that you'll think it's snowing money!"

8 He answered somewhat uninterestedly, "I've been busy working with students on their research papers and marking tests — not following the Watashaw business at all, I'm afraid. You say the demonstration went well and you're satisfied?"

9 He was definitely ⋆**putting on** a chill. We were friends now, but obviously he was still **peeved** whenever he was reminded that I had doubted that his theory could work. And he was using its success to ⋆**rub my nose in** the realization that I had been wrong. A man with a string of degrees after his name is just as human as anyone else. I had **needled** him pretty hard that first time.

10 "I'm satisfied," I acknowledged. "I was wrong. The formulas work beautifully. Come over and see my file of documents on it if you want a boost for your **ego**. Now let's see the formula for

full member 正式会员
contractual obligation 合同义务
lure 诱惑
inert 惰性的
cantankerous 脾气坏的
car-load 满载（形容数量多）
to the hilt 完全地，彻底地
grant 助学金
put on 装出，刻意表现
peeve 恼怒
rub sb's nose in 揭人伤疤，提醒
needle 刺激，激怒
ego 自尊

stopping it."

11 He sounded cheerful again. "I didn't ★**complicate** that organization with negatives. I wanted it to grow. It falls apart naturally when it stops growing for more than two months. It's like the great stock boom before an economic crash. Everyone in it is ★**prosperous** as long as the prices just keep going up and new buyers come into the market, but they all know what would happen if it stopped growing. You remember, we built in as one of the ★**incentives** that the members know they are going to lose if membership stops growing. Why, if I tried to stop it now, they'd cut my throat."

12 I remembered the drive and **frenzy** of the crowd in the one early meeting I had seen. They probably would.

13 "No," he continued. "We'll just let it **play out** to the end of its **tether** and die of old age."

14 "When will that be?"

15 "It can't grow past the female population of the town. There are only so many women in Watashaw, and some of them don't like sewing."

16 The graph on the desk before me began to look **sinister**. Surely Caswell must have made some **provision** for —

17 "You ★**underestimate** their **ingenuity**," I said into the phone. "Since they wanted to expand, they didn't stick to sewing. They went from general charity to social welfare schemes to something that's pretty close to an incorporated government. The name is now the Watashaw Mutual Trade and Civic Development Corporation, and they're filing an application to change it to Civic Property **Pool** and Social **Dividend**, membership contractual, open to all. That social dividend sounds like a **Technocrat climbed on the band wagon**, eh?"

18 While I spoke, I carefully added another red star to the curve above the thousand member level, checking with the newspaper

complicate 使复杂化
prosperous 富足的
incentive 诱因，动机
frenzy 狂热
play out 发生，展开
tether 山穷水尽
sinister 凶险的
provision 预备
underestimate 低估
ingenuity 创造力
pool 公用资源或资金
dividend 股息，红利
Technocrat 技术专家政治论者
climb on the band wagon 见风使舵

that still lay open on my desk. The curve was definitely some sort of **log curve** now, growing more rapidly with each increase.

19 "★**Leaving out** practical limitations for a moment, where does the formula say it will stop?" I asked.

20 "When you run out of people to join it. But after all, there are only so many people in Watashaw. It's a pretty small town."

21 "They've opened a branch office in New York," I said carefully into the phone, a few weeks later.

22 With my pencil, very carefully, I extended the membership curve from where it was then.

23 After the next **doubling**, the curve went almost straight up and off the page.

24 ★**Allowing for** a **lag** of **contagion** from one nation to another, depending on how much their citizens ★**intermingled**, I'd give the rest of the world about twelve years.

25 There was a long silence while Caswell probably drew the same graph in his own mind. Then he laughed weakly. "Well, you asked me for a demonstration."

26 That was as good an answer as any. We got together and had lunch in a bar, if you can call it lunch. The movement we started will expand ★**by hook or by crook**, by **seduction** or by **bribery** or by **propaganda** or by conquest, but it will expand. And maybe a total world government will be a fine thing — until it hits **the end of** its **rope** in twelve years or so.

27 What happens then, I don't know.

28 But I don't want anyone to ★**pin that on me**. From now on, if anyone asks me, I've never heard of Watashaw.

log curve 对数曲线
leave out 省去，不考虑
double 翻倍
allow for 考虑到，顾及
lag 滞后
contagion 传播，蔓延
intermingle 混合，混杂
by hook or by crook 千方百计地，不择手段地
seduction 诱惑
bribery 贿赂
propaganda 宣传
the end of rope 穷途末路
pin sth. on sb. 归咎，怪罪

Developing Ideas

Task Work in groups and discuss the following questions.

1. What happened to the club six months later?
2. What was the result of the demonstration of professor Caswell?
3. When will the snowball effect stop?
4. What lessons can be drawn from the story of Watashaw in terms of the balance between growth and ethical responsibility within organizations?
5. What are the long-term implications of the Watashaw experiment on the personal and professional lives of the protagonists, including Professor Caswell, Mr. Halloway, and Mrs. Searles, the tall woman?
6. How does Professor Caswell's unwavering belief in his formulas and the success of the Watashaw experiment challenge traditional notions of academic research and its impact on real-world outcomes?

Using Language

Task 1 Learn the word formation from the table. Complete the sentences with the correct form of the words in the table.

Word	Prefix	Root	Suffix
prospect **provision**	pro- 前，提前	spect 看 vis 看，查	/ +ion 名词缀
incorporate **incentive**	in- 进入，向内	corpor 团体 cent 唱歌	+ate 使……，动词缀 +ive ……的，名词缀、形容词缀
privilege	privi- = priv- 单个	lege 法律	/
prosperous	pro- 很多	sper 希望	+ous ……的，形容词缀
underestimate	under- 在……下，次于	estimate 估计，预测	/
intermingle	inter- 互相	mingle 混合	/
complicate	com- 全部	plic 重叠，重复	+ate 使……，动词缀

1. The successful implementation of renewable energy strategy holds great ____________ for a sustainable future.
2. Having access to quality education is a ____________ for children born in this district.
3. We have ____________ all the latest safety features into the design to produce the high-quality automobile.
4. At the international conference, participants from various countries ____________, exchanging ideas and experiences to foster a sense of global collaboration.
5. It is unwise to ____________ the determination and resilience of individuals facing adversity.
6. The instructions for assembling the furniture were so ____________ that I had to seek help from a professional.
7. Offering financial ____________ can be a powerful motivator for employees to exceed their targets and achieve exceptional results.
8. It is our belief that improvements in health care will lead to a stronger, more ____________ economy.

Task 2 Complete sentences with the correct form of the phrases in the box.

pin ... on	allow for	by hook or by crook	rub one's nose in
leave out	to the hilt	file an application	put on

1. Determined to achieve his goal, he vowed to succeed ____________, refusing to let any obstacle stand in his way.
2. When planning a project, it is important to ____________ unexpected delays or obstacles that may arise along the way.
3. The detective had a prediction but lacked concrete evidence to ____________ the crime ____________ the suspect, leading to a challenging investigation.
4. I will ____________ with the university admissions office to pursue a degree in computer science.
5. It is impolite and hurtful to ____________ children's past mistakes, as it can make them lose their confidence.
6. In copying this document, you have to be careful not to ____________ any words.
7. He embraced his new role as team captain ____________, leading by example, inspiring his teammates, and giving his absolute best in every game.
8. She ____________ a brave face and smiled, hiding her inner confusion as she pretended that everything was fine.

Task 3 Translate the paragraph into Chinese.

By looking at a spot on a leopard, the whole animal may be visualized while by observing a single drop of water, immensity of the ocean can be revealed, thus indicating we may divine the whole from a part. Pilot projects are not only crucial tasks of reform but also important methods of reform. It is essential to firmly establish a comprehensive perspective on reform, with top-level design based on the overall situation and grassroots exploration reflecting the broader picture. Both levels should explore boldly and engage actively, thus giving full play to the demonstration, breakthrough, and driving role of pilot projects in overall reform. It is necessary to carefully plan and implement various reform pilot projects, adhering to the principles of emancipating the mind, seeking truth from facts, encouraging exploration, and daring to practice. We should dare to think, dare to do, dare to explore, and dare to try. Therefore, replicable and scalable experiences and practices can be generated and reforms in various areas can be promoted.

Watching, Listening and Doing

Part 3

Watching and Doing

Task 1 Scan the QR code to watch the video clip "The Life Story of Katherine MacLean (Ⅰ)" and fill in the blanks.

SCAN ME!

Katherine Anne MacLean, born on January 22, 1925, was an American science fiction author best known for her short stories of the 1950s which examined the impact of technological advances on [1]____________ and society.

Brian Aldiss noted that she could "do the hard stuff magnificently", while Theodore Sturgeon observed that she "generally starts from a base of [2]____________, or rationalizes psi phenomena (特异现象) with beautifully finished logic". Although her stories have been included in numerous anthologies and a few have had radio and television [3]____________, *The Diploids and Other Flights of Fancy* (1962) is her only collection of short fiction.

Born in Glen Ridge, New Jersey, MacLean [4]____________ on mathematics and science in high school. At the time her earliest stories were being [5]____________ in 1949-50, she received a B.A. in economics from Barnard College (1950), followed by postgraduate studies in psychology at various universities. Her marriage to Charles Dye ended in [6]____________ a year later. She married David Mason in 1956. Their son, Christopher Dennis Mason, was born in 1957, and they divorced in 1962.

MacLean taught [7]____________ at the University of Maine and creative writing at the Free University of Portland. Over decades, she has continued to write while employed in a wide variety of jobs — as book [8]____________, economic graphanalyst (图形分析员), editor, EKG technician, food analyst, laboratory technician in penicillin research, nurse's aide, office manager and payroll bookkeeper (记账员), photographer, pollster, public relations, publicist and store [9]____________.

It was while she worked as a laboratory technician in [10]____________ that she began writing science fiction. Strongly influenced by Ludwig von Bertalanffy's General Systems Theory, her fiction has often demonstrated a remarkable [11]____________ in scientific advancements.

SCAN ME!

Task 2 Scan the QR code to watch the video clip "The Life Story of Katherine MacLean (Ⅱ)" and fill in the blanks.

Throughout her career, she has explored themes of [1]____________, societal evolution, and the impact of technology, establishing herself as a [2]____________ force within the science fiction community.

After completing her undergraduate studies in economics at Barnard College in 1947, she delved into science fiction, publishing her first short story, "[3]____________", in *Astounding Science Fiction* magazine in 1949. This marked the beginning of MacLean's illustrious writing career. Some of her notable works include [4]____________, *The Snowball Effect*, and *Games*. Her stories have been published in various science fiction magazines and anthologies.

Known for her meticulous research and attention to scientific detail, MacLean's stories often explore the [5]____________ of technological advancements on humanity. Her works are characterized by their focus on the psychological and emotional impact of scientific progress, as well as the [6]____________ that arise from the intersection of humans and machines. This thematic exploration sets her apart from many of her [7]____________ and has cemented her legacy as a pioneer of speculative fiction.

Throughout her career, MacLean's writings have gained critics' praise and numerous honors. She was [8]____________ nominated for the prestigious Hugo Award, first in 1953 for *The Snowball Effect* and again in 1955 for her novella *The Man Who Staked the Stars*. Although she did not win either time, her nominations serve as a testament to her significant [9]____________ to the science fiction genre.

In addition to her short stories, MacLean also penned a few novels, including *The Missing Man* (1975) and *Cosmic Checkmate* (1979). These longer works allowed her to expand her [10]____________ and further explore her [11]____________. While she may not have been as prolific as some of her contemporaries, MacLean's impact on science fiction remains [12]____________.

Despite her success and influence, MacLean's writing career experienced a [13]____________ in the [14]____________, as she shifted her focus to other interests. She became involved in the field of transpersonal psychology and pursued a career as a counselor and educator. Nevertheless, her earlier works continue to captivate readers and inspire new generations of science fiction authors.

Katherine MacLean's contributions to science fiction have solidified her position as a [15]____________ writer in the genre. Her ability to blend scientific accuracy with thought-provoking themes and explore the depths of human consciousness has left an indelible mark on the genre. Although her writing career has spanned several decades, MacLean's impact and legacy continue to shine through her timeless stories, which remain as relevant and engaging as ever.

Listening and Doing

Task ***Scan the QR code to listen to the audio clip "Snowball Effect" and decide whether the statements are true (T) or false (F).***

SCAN ME!

1. The snowball effect describes how small actions or events can lead to significant consequences over time.
2. The snowball effect only applies to positive actions and events.
3. In business, the snowball effect refers to the gradual decrease in profits over time.
4. The snowball effect is only relevant in personal relationships and not in economic ventures.
5. The snowball effect implies that minor environmental degradation cannot lead to severe ecological damage.
6. Being mindful of our actions can help harness the power of positive snowball effects and mitigate negative ones.

Further Reading

Mini-Pedia — Trailblazing Women Authors

Katherine Anne MacLean, Octavia E. Butler and N. K. Jemisin are notable for being women in a genre historically dominated by male writers.

Octavia E. Butler (1947-2006), an acclaimed African-American science fiction writer, was born and raised in Pasadena, California. She discovered her love for writing at a young age and began crafting stories that combined elements of science fiction, fantasy, and social commentary.

Butler's works often challenged conventional narratives and pushed the boundaries of the genre. She tackled themes of race, gender, power dynamics, and the human condition, offering nuanced and complex portrayals of her characters and their struggles. Her writing was characterized by its depth, empathy, and ability to confront uncomfortable truths about society.

Some of Butler's most notable works include the *Patternist* series, the *Xenogenesis* trilogy, and the critically acclaimed novel *Kindred*. In *Kindred*, Butler explored the legacy of slavery in America by sending her modern-day protagonist back in time to the antebellum South. The novel received widespread acclaim for its unflinching portrayal of the horrors of slavery and its impact on both individuals and society. Throughout her career, Octavia Butler received numerous awards and accolades, including the Hugo, Nebula, and MacArthur Genius Grant.

N. K. Jemisin (1972-) was born in Iowa City, Iowa. She developed a passion for storytelling at an early age and began crafting her own imaginative worlds. She has been praised for her ability to seamlessly blend elements of fantasy and science fiction with insightful commentary on race, power, and social structures.

One of Jemisin's most notable achievements is her *Broken Earth* trilogy, which includes the novels *The Fifth Season*, *The Obelisk Gate*, and *The Stone Sky*. This groundbreaking series, set in a world plagued by geological upheavals, explores themes of oppression, survival, and the consequences of human actions. The trilogy received widespread acclaim and made history when each book in the series won the prestigious Hugo Award for Best Novel, making Jemisin the first author to achieve this feat.

In addition to her *Broken Earth* trilogy, Jemisin has written other critically acclaimed works, including the *Inheritance* trilogy and the *Dreamblood* duology. Her writing has been recognized with numerous awards, including the Nebula, Locus, and the nomination of World Fantasy Awards.

Answer

Unit 6

Brian Aldiss and the Evolution

Starting out

Look at the pictures and discuss the following questions.

1. Do you think humans are going towards extinction?
2. How do you think about human evolution?
3. How do you think about the influence of modern machinery on humans?
4. Would it be better if people returned to ancient times?
5. What's the implication of the moon in your culture?

Part 1

Reading and Understanding

One Blink of the Moon（Ⅰ）

1 A letter lay in the front hall under the **letter flap**, an **air mail envelope** bearing foreign stamps. Opening the door, I stood on the porch and **slit** the envelope. Mike joined me, bringing two cans of beer with him.

2 The letter was from the United States, from a cheerful and mad scholar who had visited us in the early spring. No need to go into details, but he was ★**compiling** a **definitive volume** on architectural approaches to ideas of common territory and wished to ★**incorporate** some of my work. So bright was the moon, that generous August moon — it was at its full that night — that I could read his bold, dark handwriting by its light. My **correspondent's** handwriting was **immaculate** in its **Italianate** style. His ability with a camera was rather less than his **penmanship**. He **enclosed with** the letter three photographs that he had taken when leaving. These **snaps** showed my wife and me standing with two of our children and my father (who was then living with us as we tended him in the early stages of his final illness) before the porch, between the four **Ionic columns**.

3 Because they had been taken rather distantly, these maps showed our figures as if behind bars. When I ★**puzzled** them **out** in the moonlight, looking up at the actual later version of the scene depicted, I realized that the bars were **spears of pampas** which had got in the path of the camera lens. The pale spring sun on our living room window had the effect of ★**blanking** it **out**, as if a shutter had been drawn on the inside of the window. **Over-exposure** led to a pale moonlight effect in the three views or so it appeared to me examining them by real

letter flap 信件投递袋
air mail envelope 航空信封
slit 在……上开狭长口子
compile 编写
definitive volume 最终卷
incorporate 包含，合并
correspondent 通信者
immaculate 无瑕疵的
Italianate 意大利的
penmanship 书法
enclose with 随函附上
snap 快照
Ionic column 爱奥尼柱
puzzle out 苦心思索
spear of pampas 潘帕斯草原的嫩草
blank out（使）成为空白
over-exposure 曝光过度

moonlight over my beer.

4 I passed them to Mike.

5 "You and Joyce are thin," he said. He laughed. "Did you diet over the winter?"

6 It was true that the tricks of light past and light present made both my wife and me look **etiolated**. Our children also appeared to have a **wan** passivity. Only my father, as far as I could determine, looked **hale**, ready for many more years of life. Here I was, as full of sun and wine as a grape, bursting with energy; the photographs might almost have come from the future rather than the past. Although I am not an imaginative man, a feeling of **ghostliness** overcame me, a sense of being **insubstantial**, a sense that even the house was insubstantial. Of a sudden, I was impatient with Mike's company, and wanted to see my wife and children again.

7 We walked in the moonlit garden, collecting vegetables. They were dying, killed by a long drought which the recent downpour had come too late to **mend**.

8 "I don't ★**feel inclined to** sleep in the house tonight," I said.

9 He asked me where we should go. I pointed towards the south where, over the stone wall and the neighboring fields a line of hills could distantly be seen.

10 "We'll go on the downs, enjoy one last night sleeping in the open."

11 We set out after a supper of bread, spring onions, lemon radish, cheese, and wine. The downs were no more than twelve miles away by road, or rather by the many **winding** roads which lay between our house and the hills. There **byways** formed a network between the main **arterial** road and the high ground, linking the villages whose names stood frequent signposts: Kingstone Coomhe, Lettourne Bowers, Waldrist Magna, Bayhourne, Coxford Bassett, Coxford Regis, Piddlewalton. Upper and Lower

etiolate 使变苍白
wan 苍白的，没有血色的
hale （尤指老人）健壮的
ghostliness 幽灵般的东西
insubstantial 虚幻的
mend 修补
feel/be inclined to 有……倾向
wind 蜿蜒
byway 小路
arterial（道路或铁路）干线的，主干的

Trindle, Childrey, Chaddle, Chorney, and the two Beauchamps, Compton and Winslow: names that were music in the swelling score of the countryside as it rose to its grand conclusion on the Waldrist Downs. We climbed Pulpit Hill and were upon the brow of the world.

12 Stopping the car and climbing out, we entered another age. Whilst the villages we had passed through had appeared lifeless, from the Down another picture emerged. We looked across a vale that was fairly seemed with lights. For anyone who cared, each village was ★identifiable as a patch of illumination in the night, as far as the distant towns of Didingford and Wanbury. Where we stood, no artificial lighting existed and Light itself reigned. Nothing stirred.

13 The great moon shone down from a southern sky unflawed by cloud, making that sky a shield. All about us, it created silence over the land.

14 I took binoculars from the car and scanned the dark country below us, seeking a glimpse of my home. Dark clumps of trees, sodium lighting along a road, helped me pick it out. A gleam flashed through the eyepieces; the window which in the photographs appeared shuttered gave out a silver beam, reflected from the moon behind us. I read it as a signal; but what the signal meant I could not say.

15 I turned back towards the car. It had gone. My cousin had gone.

16 For a moment I believed myself blinded by the beam which bad ★penetrated my eye. But the Down was still visible, the moon sill steady in the sky.

17 Yet a change had come over them too. The moon appeared more flat, as if its craters and mountains had been ★obliterated, the sky more dark, the great hog-back of the Down more pallid, almost as if I ★were embedded in some faulty new photographic

swelling score 不断增长的音量
brow 额头，眉头
whilst 虽然
vale 山谷
identifiable 可辨认的
illumination 照明，光源
reign 统治
stir 搅动
binoculars 双筒望远镜
clump 树丛
sodium lighting 钠灯照明
gleam 微光，闪烁
eyepiece（望远镜的）目镜
beam 光线
bad 非常，很
penetrate 穿透，渗透
crater（由于爆炸或巨物撞击形成的）坑
obliterate 消灭，清除
hog-back 陡峻的拱地
pallid（尤指因病）苍白的
be embedded in 被嵌入

process being carried out ★**on an astronomical scale**.

18 Before I could recover from my astonishment, I saw that people approaching along the wide track into which I had driven our vehicle. That track over the **chalk**, I should say, was the Ridgeway and had existed since **time immemorial**. It formed an unhealing scar across the entire land, from the wild mountains in the west, down to the river **estuary** in the east. Throughout its length, it kept as smooth as possible to high ground, as if the first **transhumance** peoples who **trod** it, along with their sheep and thin mistress cattle, ★**deliberately** chose country that would remain — thanks to the thinness of its soils — forever uninhabited.

19 The group coming from the west showed as a dark, indeterminate feature against the **pallor** of moon-washed ground. They approached in silence.

20 As they emerged from **translucent** night, I saw they were many in number and I ★**instinctively** shrank back against a **hawthorn** bush growing in the hedge by the road. Among the walkers were cars and other machines, all moving silently and ★**at** walking **pace**. The first figures came level with one: they proved to be the leaders of a vast **caravan** stretching back down the old green truck as far as eye could see.

21 The machines that accompanied them were familiar. There were cars and lorries, as well as machines which it was not inappropriate to find in country districts, such as **harvesters** and **balers**. Other machines were more out of place. There were **cranes** and many other objects not normally seen on the move. Great dams moved by like waves of concrete.

on an astronomical scale 以天文调光摄影模式
chalk 白垩岩
time immemorial 远古时代
estuary 河口
transhumance 畜牧季移
trod 踩，踏
deliberately 故意地
pallor 苍白
translucent 半透明的
instinctively 本能地
hawthorn 山楂树
at ... pace 以……速度
caravan 大篷车，旅行队
harvester 收割机
baler 压捆机
crane 起重机

Developing Ideas

Task 1 Summarize the story and complete the table.

PARAS 1-6	By the light of the [1]____________, I looked carefully at three [2]____________ taken by [3]____________ from [4]____________. ● The photos looked abnormal in color because the [5]____________ had the blur effect and [6]____________ led to a [7]____________ effect. ● The people in the photos looked weird — my wife and I looked [8]____________; our children appeared to have [9]____________; only my father, in his final [10]____________, looked [11]____________, ready for many more years of life. ● I got a feeling of [12]____________ and [13]____________, which creates an atmosphere of [14]____________ and [15]____________.
PARAS 7-15	We decided to go on [16]____________ for one last night. ● The downs were [17]____________ away from my house. We drove on the many [18]____________ and [19]____________, along which there were many [20]____________ with beautiful [21]____________, but [22]____________. ● In the night, each village was [23]____________ as a patch of [24]____________ across the vale, but where we stood, [25]____________ existed except [26]____________ itself. ● When we got there, I received a [27]____________ from the moon while [28]____________ suddenly disappeared.
PARAS 16-21	A vast caravan of [29]____________ emerged as a dark, indeterminate feature against the pallor of moon-washed ground and [30]____________ towards me. *Can you guess what the caravan represents and how it will change?

Task 2 Decide whether the statements are true (T) or false (F) according to the passage.

☐ 1. The photos of my family were taken on a full moon night in August.

☐ 2. The items looking like bars in the photos were actually spears of pampas.

☐ 3. The health condition of my family appeared to be weird because of the tricks of light past and light present.

☐ 4. From the view on the down, the villages we had just passed still appeared lifeless.

☐ 5. The moon gave me a signal by casting its light on the window appearing shuttered in the photos.

☐ 6. The people were along with their sheep and thin mistress cattle.

Using Language

Task 1 Complete the table with the correct form of the words given. Then complete the sentences with the correct form of the words in the table.

Verb	Noun	Adjective	Adverb
compile			
incorporate			
		insubstantial	
		identifiable	
penetrate			
obliterate			
			deliberately
			instinctively

1. They have spent years of work ____________ the reference book for postgraduates.
2. Many of your suggestions have been ____________ into our final plan for the development of our company.
3. The jewelry in my dream is ____________ and nothing was left when I woke up.
4. ____________ as kitties, these little ones curved into balls on the ground.
5. Without protective clothing, the harmful radiation will ____________ your skin.
6. Her memory of her hometown has been ____________ by time, and she will no longer come back.
7. Two strong men silently stalked me on my way home so I ____________ walked faster to avoid potential danger.
8. I ____________ reserved this room for you, you will be comfortable this summer because it is the only room with air conditioning.

Task 2 Complete the sentences with the correct form of the phrases in the box.

puzzle ... out	blank ... out	be inclined to
be embedded in	on an ... scale	at ... pace

1. No matter how hard it is, you should try to ___________ those feelings ___________ and start a new life.
2. I was not ___________ believe his message any longer because he cheated me of my money last month.
3. My cousin spent a whole night trying to ___________ why he could not get any recognition from his manager.
4. To achieve environmental protection of the whole world, the coal industry should be replaced by the clean energy industry ___________ international ___________.
5. The sword was ___________ the magical stone and I had been trying pretty hard to pull it out but failed at last.
6. Please don't try to hurry me. I can only climb ___________ a slow ___________, or I will get quite breathless.

Task 3 Translate the sentences into Chinese.

1. When I puzzled them out in the moonlight, looking up at the actual later version of the scene depicted, I realized that the bars were spears of pampas which had got in the path of the camera lens.

____

____

____

2. Throughout its length, it kept as smooth as possible to high ground, as if the first transhumance peoples who trod it, along with their sheep and thin mistress cattle, deliberately chose country that would remain — thanks to the thinness of its soils — forever uninhabited.

____

____

____

Task 4 Translate the paragraph into English.

如今，人们与手机形影不离，但有些人却饱受电话恐惧症的困扰，其特征表现为拨打或接听电话时产生强烈的恐惧或焦虑。患有电话恐惧症的人在使用电话时可能会出现心跳加速、出汗、颤抖和呼吸困难等症状。由于手机在很大程度上促进了交流，这种恐惧可能会对个人生活和职业生涯产生许多不良影响。例如，错过同事、客户或主管的重要电话可能会导致错失机会、误解，甚至有可能使职业受挫。因电话恐惧症而痛苦的人可能会避开社交活动、聚会，甚至与工作有关的讨论，从而落到社交孤立和沟通障碍的地步。鉴于电话恐惧症的严重影响，它确实可以被视为一种社会问题，需要理解、同情和潜在干预。

Part 2

Appreciating and Comprehending

One Blink of the Moon (Ⅱ)

1 This ★**inexplicable** tide of human and inhuman continued steadily forward, moving in front of me from western horizon to eastern, always with the **brazen** moon behind it keeping it in **silhouette**. I watched a moving **frieze**.

2 Staring in a kind of **stupefaction**, I realized after a longtime that the nature of the machinery was changing. It was growing bigger. Bigger, and more complex. Fewer of the items could I comprehend. The people were also changing, although less dramatically. They walked with a more automatic **gait**, scarcely swinging their arms; I **fancied** too that they were all now dressed more uniformly. Before this (the realization ★**dawned upon** me), a few of them had been dancing.

3 This **implacable** caravan grew thicker. The entire Down became covered by black moving masses in which people could be distinguished progressing **sluggishly** at the bases of **towering** machinery. All the time the moon hung ★**stationary** in the sky above us. Everything in nature was unmoving.

4 The events of the previous week had made me harmonious to an unusual degree with the world of which I formed such a small part. I felt myself ★**in tune with** my present surroundings. My cousin had returned home through Europe, visiting many of its grander natural features, among them the **volcanic pile**, growing slowly from a period long before man emerged on the planet, which we call Mount Etna. Mike had been ★**eloquent** about this enormous **abscess** on the earth's surface, which the great Lyell described as a monument set to impress all the peoples of Europe with the vast distances of time.

5 Taken though I was with Mike's account of Etna, I still

inexplicable 费解的
brazen 黄铜色的
silhouette（浅色背景衬托出的）暗色轮廓
frieze 饰带
stupefaction 麻木状态
gait 步法，步态
fancy 认为
dawn upon 领悟，想到
implacable 势不可挡的
sluggishly 缓慢地
towering 耸立的，高大的
stationary 静止不动的
in tune with 一致
volcanic pile 火山堆
eloquent 雄辩的，流利的
abscess 脓肿（此处指火山堆）

retained an immense respect for the distances of time as evidenced less **flamboyantly** by the downs on which I stood. For the Waldrist Downs, upon whose shallow soil I had often lain, ⋆**was composed** to a depth **of** many hundred feet of chalk made from the **carapaces** of **myriads** of tiny creatures, once alive, long dead, ⋆**bearing** ⋆**witness to** those same majestic processes which moved the minds of Lyell and Darwin, who had learned from Lyell's work.

6 I never walked on the Downs, **savoring** the sweetness of the air and of my own brief lifespan, without bearing in mind that continual double wonder: the processes of Earth and the processes of the human mind which, alone, is capable of interpreting and **rendering** Earth meaningful.

7 Now those processes were **manifesting themselves** in new way — new but not entirely strange. Well, yes, strange — but we are more familiar than we care to admit with what is strange.

8 ⋆**By degrees** the strange **procession** became familiar. Without **fatigue** I watched the unending silhouette as it dragged from veiled horizon to veiled horizon ever smaller machines, ever smaller people. The **tempo** became slower. The people marched in **leaden** step. Such was my emotional involvement that I seemed to travel about the Earth with them. I almost became part of them, as each tiny creature beneath our feet was part of the deep chalk. This I struggled against. I hated their defeat. Their **shuffling** presence was unbearable — they had lost human joy, human display. They walked under the bare sky as if imprisoned down a mine. They **enacted** a funeral of life.

9 The moon remained completely unaltered, unmoving. In time, something in the nature of the **cavalcade** altered. Slowly it dawned on me that although the machines were still increasing in size — they towered high into the sky, falling into its pale

retain 保留
flamboyantly 炫耀地
be composed of 由……构成
carapace 甲壳
myriad 无数，大量
bear witness to 证明
savor 品味
render 使变得
manifest oneself 显现
by degrees 逐渐地
procession 行列
fatigue 劳累
tempo 节奏
leaden 沉闷的
shuffle 拖着脚走
enact 举行
cavalcade 车队

face as they passed — they were becoming fewer in number. The people grew yet more *multitudinous. This was the order of things for so long that it seemed as if the procession had always been so constituted. The people became more featureless, leaning forward as if against a wind they could hardly *endure.

10 Another change at last, gradual, gradual. There was a wind in the ranks of the megamachines. Nothing but people files past, monotonous, unending, glancing neither to left nor right. They flowed like a river without meander, coming from a hidden source towards an unknown destiny.

11 In the west a black object rose. For an age, it appeared like a black doppelglänger of the stationary moon, until its approach defined its outlines more clearly. It was shaped like the Great Pyramid of Egypt, was fully a match for that monument in size. It loomed steadily up from obscurity, grinding over the crescent of Waldrist Downs, dwarfing the attendants last at its base. For the first time 1 knew fear, I was unable to flee.

12 This terrible machine grew, slicing out larger and larger segments of sky. I can still feel that thing towering closer to me forever, making its own night within night. It was horned at the top with bristling horns.

13 It made no noise. Yet its monstrousness crested a kind of visual thunder.

14 The moon was again revealed. Sane, mellow, familiar, bland, it shed its radiance as before. Now there was a mere trickle of people on which it shone.

15 And those people made their obscure journey bent almost double. Some threw up their arms in supplication. Some progressed on hands and knees.

16 This *degradation seemed no worse than the robot — like march I had witnessed long before. Yet I *grieved

multitudinous 众多的
constitute 组成，构成
endure 忍受
megamachine 巨型机器
file 排成一行（行走）
monotonous 单调的
meander 曲径
doppelglänger 幽灵
loom（庞大模糊物）赫然耸现
obscurity 黑暗，昏暗
grind 碾压
crescent 新月
dwarf 使显得矮小
horn 把……装上角
bristle 竖起，耸起
crest 达到顶点
mellow 柔和的，圆润的
bland 温和的
shed 散发出（光）
a trickle of 一小股细流的
supplication 祈求，恳求
degradation 堕落，退化
grieve 悲伤

17 The **stooped** figures became fewer. A numb feeling of relief struggled up in my being — to be **quenched** by **anguish**. Was this, I asked myself, the end of the great procession, the end of man's journey? **Crippled**. dumb, degraded, the last silhouette passed.

18 But no more figures were on their way. A few more curved backs, then — a group, a group dancing! They came towards me down the ancient trackway. They **pranced** over the **cretaceous** hill. Although their movements were clumsy, they expressed joy — or did I read my own joy into them. I believe not.

19 More dancers arrived. They were always in groups, some small, some larger. Their costumes grew more decorative, their movements more graceful, their steps more **intricate**, so that I **strained my ears**, listening for a **phantom** music. How I would have loved to hear that music.

20 A sort of melody began to reach me, a music of action and graceful limbs. The human **panorama** was free now. Without its machines, it was recapturing something of the **spontaneity** that early man must have possessed in the world's wilds. Before my eyes new languages developed, **couched** in **nudity** and ***elaborate** dress, in **choreography** and liquid gesture. For the first time, the frieze took on a genuine light-heartedness.

21 As time wore on, that light-heartedness grew to something more intense. A fresh mode was evolving; its rhythms were different from anything I knew. The people themselves were unknown, as if their bodies had developed new joints, fresh qualities of action. Their minds and thoughts had developed beyond my understanding.

22 One thing did awaken my sympathetic comprehension. The beautiful strangers **flocking** past were accompanied by animals. Large animals and small wild or domestic, they **cavorted** among the human forms, playing a deliberate part in the ceremony.

stoop 俯身，弯腰
quench 扑灭，熄灭
anguish 痛苦
cripple 使跛足
prance 腾跃
cretaceous 白垩纪的
intricate 错综复杂的
strain one's ears 努力听
phantom 幻影，幽灵
panorama 全景
spontaneity 自发性
couch 表达
nudity 裸体
elaborate 精心制作的
choreography 编舞
flock 聚集；群集
cavort 欢跃

Monkeys and **macaws** rode on humans, men and women rode on tigers and horses.

23 This fantastic **masque** brought grave joy. Just to watch was to wish to watch forever. Indeed at the time it seemed to continue forever. It **girdled** the world. All life had united. Life was a **pageant**, slowly the players changed: some of the animal forms became large and fantastic, the **bipeds** more diverse in shape.

24 **Epochs** passed, while I could no longer comprehend what was happening. A kind of long ceremonial was played out before me, enacted by beings as like and unlike humans as **elves**. ***At length**, like elves, they were taking to low **darting** flight. The **argent** night became full of wings and **enchantments**.

macaw 金刚鹦鹉
masque 假面舞会
girdle 环绕；围绕
pageant 盛会
biped 两足动物
epoch 时代；纪元
elf 精灵
at length 最后
dart 飞奔
argent 银白色的
enchantment 魅力

Developing Ideas

Task　Work in groups and discuss the following questions.

1. What do the changing machines imply?
2. What does "They enacted a funeral of life" (para. 8) mean?
3. Why did people, cars, and machines keep moving in the story?
4. What do the dancing people and the melody represent?
5. How do you think of the people after the disappearance of the pyramid shaped machine?
6. What role does the moon play in this story?

Using Language

Task 1　Learn the word formation from the table. Complete the sentences with the correct form of the words in the table.

Word	Prefix	Root	Suffix
inexplicable	in- 否定前缀	ex 出 + plic 重叠，折叠	+able 能……的
stationary	/	stat 站 + ion 行为	+ary 形容词缀

Word	Prefix	Root	Suffix
eloquent	e- 出，外	loqu 说话	+ent 形容词缀
multitudinous	multi- 多个	itude 性质状态等	+ous 形容词缀
endure	en- 使……	dur 持久，坚硬的	/
degradation	de- 向下，降低	grade 等级	+tion 名词缀
grieve	/	griev 重 + e	/
elaborate	e- 加强	labor 劳动，工作	+ate 做，造

1. For ____________ reasons I always had the same dream that following spring.
2. This TV presenter earned a reputation in media circle for having a ready and ____________ tongue.
3. The declining film industry and the shrinking media industry is a signal of the ____________ of their culture.
4. To look more attractive, she bought this ____________ necklace for the royal banquet tonight.
5. His family ____________ a miserable existence in this small apartment before his father won the lottery.
6. Our city is a form of accumulation made up of ____________ resources such as the economy, the population, the information and so on.
7. The audience remained ____________ at the entrance until the usher led them to their seats in the second row.
8. Children from broken family are more prone to show emotional ____________ according to this teacher.

Task 2 Complete the sentences with the correct form of the phrases in the box.

dawn upon	in tune with	be composed of
bear witness to	by degrees	at length

1. The buried truth gradually began to ____________ him since he was forced to grow up too fast.
2. As time goes on, the focus of human resource management will be turned to performance management ____________.
3. Cities that have kept their historical buildings ____________ the splendid civilization of human society.
4. The police have been questioned her for two days, and ____________ they allowed her to go home.
5. She became successful because her ideas were ____________ the spirit of her age.
6. Parents agreed to accept this council which would ____________ teachers and students.

Task 3 Translate the paragraph into Chinese.

Ethics in technology encompasses various aspects. One key area is the societal impact of technology. Developers and innovators should consider the potential consequences of their creations on society at large. Ethical considerations must be integrated into the design and deployment of technologies to avoid negative outcomes such as discrimination, inequality, or job displacement. Embracing a technologically advanced future requires us to navigate the intricate relationship between technology and ethics. By proactively considering the ethical dimensions of technological advancements, we can ensure that innovation is in tune with our shared values and contributes positively to society. Balancing progress with responsible practices will pave the way for a more ethical and inclusive technological landscape.

Part 3

Watching, Listening and Doing

Watching and Doing

SCAN ME!

Task 1 Scan the QR code to watch the video clip "The Life Story of Brian Aldiss (Ⅰ)" and fill in the blanks.

Brian Aldiss, born on August 18, 1925, was a highly [1]____________ English writer known for his significant contributions to science fiction literature. Over his prolific career, which spanned several decades, Aldiss crafted a/an [2]____________ body of works encompassing novels, short stories, essays, and non-fiction, earning him widespread acclaim and numerous awards.

Aldiss was born in Dereham, Norfolk, England. From an early age, he displayed a keen interest in literature and storytelling. As a child, he discovered the magazine *Astounding Science-Fiction* and [3]____________ himself in the works of science fiction writers like H. G. Wells, Robert Heinlein, and Philip K. Dick, sparking his [4]____________ and igniting his passion for science fiction.

At the age of eighteen, Aldiss joined the British Army during World War Ⅱ, serving in Burma and the Far East as part of the Royal Signals Regiment. His [5]____________ experiences greatly influenced his writing and provided him with firsthand [6]____________ into the human conditions and the influence of technology on society, themes that would appear throughout his literary career. After the war, Aldiss worked as a [7]____________, which further inspired his writing. In the [8]____________, he began publishing short stories in science fiction magazines, quickly gaining recognition for his imaginative concepts and thought-provoking narratives.

SCAN ME!

Task 2 Scan the QR code to watch the video clip "The Life Story of Brian Aldiss (Ⅱ)" and fill in the blanks.

In 1955, Aldiss published his first novel, *The Brightfount Diaries*, which marked a [1]____________ in his career. The success of this novel propelled him to the forefront of science fiction writing. In late 1950s, his earnings from writing matched his wages in the bookshop and he became a [2]____________ science fiction writer.

Aldiss continued to publish acclaimed novels such as *Hothouse* in 1962, *Report on Probability A* in 1968, and *Frankenstein Unbound* in [3]____________. *Frankenstein Unbound* is a story about a Time-Traveling scientist who accidentally travels back to the early 19th century and encounters Victor Frankenstein and his monster, grapples with the [4] ___________ surrounding the creation of life and the potential dangers it poses. The novel has been praised for its imaginative blending of genres and its exploration of [5] ___________.

His writing revealed a deep understanding of human nature, often exploring themes of evolution, morality, and the impact of [6] ___________ on society. He was [7] ___________ with the New Wave movement, which had a significant impact on the science fiction genre, [8] ___________ traditional tropes and conventions of science fiction and tried to push the [9] ___________ of the genre and explore new themes and narrative techniques.

Beyond his literary achievements, Aldiss was known for his boundless enthusiasm and [10] ___________ for science fiction. He actively participated in conventions, [11] ___________, and workshops, sharing his knowledge and inspiring future generations of writers. His mentorship and [12] ___________ left an indelible mark on aspiring authors, fostering a sense of community and fostering growth within the science fiction community.

Brian Aldiss's influence [13] ___________ far beyond the boundaries of the science fiction genre. His pioneering work and inventive imagination broke new ground, pushing the boundaries of what science fiction could achieve. His profound [14] ___________ on the human condition and society continue to resonate with readers worldwide.

Listening and Doing

SCAN ME!

Task ***Scan the QR code to listen to the audio clip "Technology and Emotions" and decide whether the statements are true (T) or false (F).***

1. Technological advancement has a profound impact on our emotions.
2. Technology can revolutionize emotional connectivity through social media platforms.
3. The emotional connectivity on social media platforms can bridge gaps and foster a sense of belonging in an increasingly digital world.
4. Technological advancement poses no challenges to our emotional well-being.
5. As an emotional aid, technology can entirely replace human beings.
6. Safeguarding personal data and respecting emotional boundaries should be important in developing technologies.

Further Reading

Mini-Pedia — Three Literary Pioneers

Brian Aldiss, Ursula K. Le Guin and James Graham Ballard are considered pioneers in their own right. They pushed the boundaries of traditional science fiction and speculative fiction, exploring new ideas, themes and narrative structures that often challenge established norms.

Ursula K. Le Guin (1929-2018) was an American author known for her groundbreaking works in the genres of fiction and fantasy. She produced a vast body of work that explored complex themes such as gender, politics, and the human condition. Her novels, short stories, and essays challenged traditional notions of genre and pushed the boundaries of speculative fiction.

One of Le Guin's most notable contributions to literature was her radical investigation of gender roles. In her novel *The Left Hand of Darkness*, she introduced readers to a world where gender is fluid and individuals can change their sex at will. This groundbreaking work challenged societal norms, sparked discussions about nature of gender and its impact on identity, and won both Hugo Award and Nebula Award.

Beyond her literary achievements, Le Guin was also a passionate advocate for social and environmental justice. Her works often addressed themes of power, oppression, and the importance of understanding and respecting the natural world. Her essays and speeches demonstrated her commitment to creating a more equitable and sustainable society.

James Graham Ballard (1930-2009) was a British writer, widely regarded as one of the most influential and innovative science fiction authors in the 20th century. His works often explore the intersection of technology, psychology, and the human condition. He is best known for his dystopian(反乌托邦)novels, which depict a world in which the boundaries between reality and fantasy are blurred.

One of Ballard's most famous works is *Crash*, published in 1973. It explores the special fascination with car crashes and the psychological effects of technology on human desire. It pushed the boundaries of conventional literature and sparked intense debates about the relationship between humans and machines. Another iconic work by Ballard is *The Drowned World*, which depicts a future where rising sea levels have transformed the Earth into a tropical wasteland. This novel, along with others like *High-Rise* and *Concrete Island*, showcased Ballard's ability to create vivid and unsettling visions of the future.

Throughout his career, Ballard consistently pushed the boundaries of science fiction, blending elements of surrealism and psychological exploration. His contributions to literature and his ability to push the boundaries of imagination make him a true icon in the science fiction genre.

Answer

Unit 7

Brain Aldiss and His Time Travel

Starting out

Look at the pictures and discuss the following questions.

1. Have you ever heard of Jurassic Era? Are you interested in it?
2. If you could time travel back to the Jurassic Era, what would you most like to do?
3. Are you up for the challenge of wilderness survival?
4. Imagine what your biggest challenge would be if you stayed in the wild alone.
5. Do you believe that humans can conquer nature?

Part 1

Reading and Understanding

Poor Little Warrior (Ⅰ)

1 You crawled **heedlessly** through the mud among the willows, through the little ⋆**primitive** flowers with petals as green and brown as a football field, through the beauty-lotion mud. You peered out at the creature **sprawling** among the reeds, its body as graceful as a sock full of sand. There it lay, letting the gravity **cuddle** it **nappy-damp** to the marsh, running its big rabbit-hole **nostrils** a foot above the grass in a sweeping semicircle, in a snoring search for more sausagy reeds. It was beautiful: here horror had reached its limits, come full circle and finally disappeared up its own **sphincter**. Its eyes gleamed with the liveliness of a week-dead **corpse's** big toe, and its **compost** breath and the fur in its ⋆**crude aural cavities** were particularly to be **recommended** to anyone who might otherwise have felt inclined to speak lovingly of the work of Mother Nature.

2 But as you, little mammal with opposed digit and .65 self-loading, semi-automatic, dual-**barrelled**, digitally-computed, ⋆**telescopically** sighted, rustless, high-powered rifle gripped in your otherwise-defenceless paws, slide along under the bygone willows, what ⋆**primarily** attracts you is the thunder lizard's hide. It gives off a smell as deeply ⋆**resonant** as the bass note of a piano. It makes the elephant's **epidermis** look like a sheet of **crinkled** lavatory paper. It is grey as the **Viking** seas, draught-deep as cathedral foundations. What contact possible to bone could allay the fever of that flesh? Over it **scamper** — you can see them from here! — the little brown **lice** that live in those grey walls and canyons, gay as ghosts, cruel as crabs. If one of them jumped on you, it would very likely break your back. And when one of those **parasites** stops to **cock** its leg against one of

heedlessly 若无其事地
primitive 原始的，简陋的
sprawl 蠕动
cuddle 怀抱
nappy-damp 湿漉漉的
nostril 鼻孔
sphincter 括约肌
corpse 尸体
compost 堆肥，混合物
crude 粗糙的
aural cavity 耳腔
recommend 劝告，推荐
barrel 枪管
telescopically 可伸缩地
primarily 主要地，首要地
resonant 共鸣的，洪亮的
epidermis 表皮
crinkled 起皱的
Viking 维京，北欧海盗
scamper 蹦蹦跳跳
lice 虱子
parasite 寄生虫
cock 翘起

the bronto's vertebrae, you can see it carries in its turn its own crop of easy-livers, each as big as a lobster, for you're near now, oh, so near that you can hear the monster's primitive heart-organ knocking, as the ventricle keeps miraculous time with the auricle.

3 Time for listening to the oracle is past: you're beyond the stage for omens, you're now headed in for the kill, yours or his; *superstition has had its little day for today, from now on only this windy nerve of yours, this shaky conglomeration of muscle entangled *untraceably beneath the sweat-shiny carapace of skin, this bloody little urge to slay the dragon, is going to answer all your orisons.

4 You could shoot now. Just wait till that tiny steam-shovel head pauses once again to gulp down a quarry-load of bulrushes, and with one inexpressibly vulgar bang you can show the whole indifferent Jurassic world that it's standing looking down the business end of evolution's sex-shooter. You know why you pause, even as you pretend not to know why you pause; that old worm conscience, long as a baseball pitch, long-lived as a tortoise, is at work; through every sense it slides, more monstrous than the serpent. Through the passions: saying here is a sitting duck, O Englishman! Through the intelligence: whispering that boredom, the kite-hawk who never feeds, will settle again when the task is done. Through the nerves: sneering that when the adrenalin currents cease to flow the vomiting begins. Through the maestro behind the retina: *plausibly forcing the beauty of the view upon you.

5 Spare us that poor old slipper-slopper of a word, beauty; holy mum, is this a travelogue, nor are we out of it? Perched now on this titanic creature's back, we see a round dozen — and folks, let me stress that round — of gaudily plumaged birds, exhibiting between them all the colour you might expect to find on lovely,

bronto (brontosaurus) 雷龙
vertebrae 椎骨
ventricle 心室
auricle 心耳
oracle 神谕
omen 预兆
superstition 迷信
conglomeration 混合物
entangle 缠绕
untraceably 无法追踪地
carapace 表层
orison 祈祷
gulp down 大口大口地吃
bulrush 芦苇，灯芯草
vulgar 本土的，粗俗的
Jurassic 侏罗纪的
adrenalin 肾上腺素
maestro 大师，大音乐家
retina 视网膜
plausibly 合理地，似真地
slipper-slopper 混乱（使用）
travelogue 旅行纪录片
perch 栖息，鲈鱼
gaudily 华丽地
plumage 翅膀，鸟类羽毛

fabled **Copacabana Beach**. They're so round because they feed from the droppings that fall from the rich man's table. Watch this lovely shot now! See the bronto's tail lift ... Oh, lovely, yep, a couple of **hyrinksful** at least ★**emerging from** his **nether** end. That sure was a beauty, folks, delivered straight from consumer to consumer. The birds are fighting over it now. Hey, you, there's enough to go round, and anyhow, you're round enough already ... And nothing to do now but hop back up onto the old **rump** steak and wait for the next round. And now as the sun sinks in the Jurassic West, we say "Fare well on that diet ...".

6 No, you're ★**procrastinating**, and that's a life work. Shoot the beast and put it out of your agony. Taking your courage in your hands, you raise it to shoulder level and **squint down** its sights. There is a terrible report; you are half stunned. Shakily, you look about you. The monster still **munches**, relieved to have broken enough wind to **unbecalm** the Ancient Mariner.

7 Angered (or is it some subtler emotion?), you now burst from the bushes and confront it, and this exposed condition is typical of the straits into which your consideration for yourself and others continually **pitches** you. Consideration? Or again something subtler? Why should you be confused just because you come from a confused civilization? But that's a point to deal with later, if there is a later, as these two **hog-wallow** eyes **pupilling** you all over from spitting distance tend to dispute. Let it not be by jaws alone, O monster, but also by huge hooves and, if convenient to yourself, by mountainous rollings upon me! Let death be a saga, **sagacious**, **Beowulfate**.

8 Quarter of a mile distant is the sound of a dozen hippos springing **boisterously** in **gymslips** from the ancestral mud, and next second a **walloping** great tail as long as Sunday and as thick as Saturday night comes slicing over your head. You duck as duck you must, but the beast missed you anyway because it

Copacabana Beach 科帕卡巴纳海滩
hyrinksful 干草堆一样的
emerge from 从……出现
nether 下面的
rump 尾部，臀部
procrastinate 拖延
squint down 向下瞄准
munch 用力咀嚼
unbecalm 不再平静
pitch 扔
hog-wallow 像猪一样的
pupil 瞳孔
sagacious 精明的
Beowulfate 英雄般的
boisterously 喧闹地
gymslip 光滑的泥潭
wallop 猛击，痛打

so happens that its coordination is *no better than yours would be if you had to wave the Woolworth Building at a tarsier. This done, it seems to feel it has done its duty by itself. It forgets you. You just wish you could forget yourself as easily; that was, after all, the reason you had to come the long way here. Get Away From It All, said the time travel brochure, which meant for you getting away from Claude Ford, a husbandman as *futile as his name with a terrible wife called Maude. Maude and Claude Ford. Who could not adjust to themselves, to each other, or to the world they were born in. It was the best reason in the as-it-is-at-present-constituted world for coming back here to shoot giant saurians — if you were fool enough to think that one hundred and fifty million years either way made an ounce of difference to the muddle of thoughts in a man's cerebral vortex.

no better than 几乎等于
tarsier 眼镜猴
brochure 小册子
futile 徒劳的
saurian 蜥蜴类
muddle 混沌
cerebral vortex 大脑涡流

Developing Ideas

Task 1 Summarize the story and complete the table.

PARAS 1-2	The vivid descriptions of the creature — [1]________ based on the protagonist's observation. ● Its body was [2]________. ● Its nostrils were [3]________ and like [4]________, which were extremely horrible when their shape [5]________. ● Its eyes [6]________. ● Its breath was smelly and the fur in its aural cavities was [7]________. ● Its thunder lizard's hide was of [8]________ color and terribly [9]________ compared with elephant's epidermis. ● Its parasites were as [10]________ and they were in huge size with their livers [11]________.

PARAS 3-6	The protagonist considered taking a shot at the creature, but he hesitated because of internal conflicts, various emotions and the behavior of the creature. ● He made sure he came here for [12]__________, and only his [13]__________, [14]__________ and [15]__________ mattered in this situation. ● He [16]__________ because he was afraid of the gigantic creature with [17]__________, [18]__________, [19]__________, [20]__________ and [21]__________, as he imagined at least. ● He was astonished at the scene where the [22]__________ fed on the brontosaurus droppings. ● He was [23]__________ for the creature broke wind.
PARAS 7-8	The subtler emotion urged the protagonist to confront with the brontosaurus and he finally found out the reason for [24]__________. ● The protagonist exposed himself to the beast within the [25]__________ distance and was ready for [26]__________. ● The beast gave an attack at the protagonist with [27]__________, but [28]__________. Then it went on eating and [29]__________ him. The reaction of the beast reminded the protagonist of the fact that he came to Jurassic world not for killing but for [30]__________ himself, his wife and real modern life. *Would the protagonist kill the immense beast or be killed by it?

Task 2 Decide whether the statements are true (T) or false (F) according to the passage.

☐ 1. In face of the creature, you will be defenseless without the rifle.

☐ 2. In the Jurassic world, superstition is believed to be effective.

☐ 3. The whole story is a travelogue and the protagonist described vividly.

☐ 4. You are half stunned because you have already shot the beast.

☐ 5. The beast's movements are as coordinated as those of a human.

☐ 6. Claude Ford can't adjust to the world they were born in.

Using Language

***Task 1** Complete the table with the correct form of the words given. Then complete the sentences with the correct form of the words in the table.*

Verb	Noun	Adjective	Adverb
			telescopically
			traceably
			heedlessly
procrastinate			
	superstition		
			plausibly
recommend			
		crude	

1. The first known ____________ observation of a total solar eclipse was made in France in 1706.
2. Raw materials are ____________ throughout milk production systems, which is the guarantee for the successful development.
3. They began to search the underwater cave, ____________ of time or any other consideration.
4. There are a lot of different ways to beat ____________, and everyone just needs to find a method that works well for them.
5. Some ____________ practices should be abolished as soon as possible.
6. This explanation is in agreement with the facts and it is psychologically ____________.
7. Rising ____________ oil prices mean that global demand is increasing and that can indicate the global economy is growing.
8. The American Academy of Pediatrics ____________ that children and adolescents do not use energy drinks.

Task 2 Complete the sentences with the correct form of the words and phrases in the box.

emerge from	resonant	primitive
no better than	futile	primarily

1. Protecting and defending folklore, which is the spirit home of human beings, is a widely ____________ topic in the context of globalization.
2. Does that make their years of effort ____________ and meaningless?
3. Psychologists found out human children did ____________ the chimps on the physical world tests but were considerably better at understanding the social world.
4. No agreement was likely to ____________ the week-long talks between the foreign ministers of the two countries.
5. She ____________ speaks to students in health classes, but sometimes the school will arrange for her to speak to residents in neighboring communities.
6. The African countries hoped to civilize all the ____________ tribes on the land.

Task 3 Translate the sentences into Chinese.

1. It gives off a smell as deeply resonant as the bass note of a piano. It makes the elephant's epidermis look like a sheet of crinkled lavatory paper. It is grey as the Viking seas, draught-deep as cathedral foundations.

____

____

____

2. Time for listening to the oracle is past: you're beyond the stage for omens, you're now headed in for the kill, yours or his; superstition has had its little day for today, from now on only this windy nerve of yours, this shaky conglomeration of muscle entangled untraceably beneath the sweat-shiny carapace of skin, this bloody little urge to slay the dragon, is going to answer all your orisons.

____

____

Task 4 Translate the paragraph into English.

中国积极推进生态文明建设和生物多样性保护，不断强化生物多样性主流化，实施生态保护红线制度，建立以国家公园为主体的自然保护地体系，实施生物多样性保护重大工程，实施最严格执法监管，一大批珍稀濒危物种得到有效保护，生态系统多样性、稳定性和可持续性不断增强，走出了一条中国特色的生物多样性保护之路。

(来源：习近平在《生物多样性公约》第十五次缔约方大会第二阶段高级别会议开幕式上的致辞)

Part 2

Appreciating and Comprehending

Poor Little Warrior (Ⅱ)

1 The bright birds sway, the lice **scamper** like dogs, the marsh ★**groans**, as bronto sways over and sends his little **cranium** snaking down under the **bile-bright** water in a **forage** for **roughage**. You watch this; you have never been so **jittery** before in all your jittered life, and you are counting on this **catharsis wringing** the last drop of acid fear out of your system for ever. OK, you keep saying to yourself ★**insanely** over and over, your million-dollar twenty-second century education going for nothing, OK, OK. And as you say it for the **umpteenth** time, the crazy head comes back out of the water like a **renegade** express and gazes in your direction.

2 Grazes in your direction. For as the champing jaw with its big blunt **molars** like concrete posts works up and down, you see the swamp water course out over ★**rimless** lips, lipless rims, splashing your feet and **sousing** the ground. Reed and root, stalk and stem, leaf and loam, all are intermittently visible in that **masticating maw** and, struggling, straggling or tossed among them, **minnows**, tiny **crustaceans**, frogs — all ★**destined** in that awful, jawful movement to turn into bowel movement. And as the glump-glump-glumping takes place, above it the **slime**-★**resistant** eyes again survey you.

3 These beasts live up to two hundred years, says the time travel brochure, and this beast has obviously tried to live up to that, for its gaze is centuries old, full of decades upon decades of **wallowing** in its heavyweight **thoughtlessness** until it has grown wise on **twitter-pated-ness**. For you it is like looking into a disturbing misty pool; it gives you a psychic shock, you fire off both barrels at your own reflection. Bang-bang, the dum-

scamper 蹦蹦跳跳地跑
groan 呻吟，发吱嘎声
cranium 颅骨
bile-bright 胆汁亮色的
forage 饲料
roughage 粗饲料
jittery 战战兢兢的
catharsis 宣泄
wring 消除
insanely 精神错乱地
umpteenth 第无数次的
renegade 叛徒
molar 臼齿
rimless 无边的
souse 浸湿
masticate 咀嚼
maw 嘴
minnow 小鱼
crustacean 甲壳纲动物
destined 注定的
slime 黏液
resistant 有抵抗力的
wallow 打滚，沉溺
thoughtlessness 无思想
twitter-pated-ness 交配季节的行为

dums, big as paw-paws, go.

4 With no *indecision, those century-old lights, dim and *sacred, go out. These cloisters are closed till Judgement Day. Your reflection is torn and bloodied from them forever. Over their ravaged panes nictitating membranes slide slowly upwards, like dirty sheets covering a cadaver. The jaw continues to munch slowly, as slowly the head sinks down. Slowly, a squeeze of cold reptile blood toothpastes down the wrinkled flank of one cheek. Everything is slow, a creepy Secondary Era slowness like the drip of water, and you know that if you had been in charge of creation you would have found some medium less heart-breaking than Time to stage it all in.

5 Never mind! Quaff down your beakers, lords, Claude Ford has *slain a harmless creature. Long live Claude the Clawed!

6 You watch breathless as the head touches the ground, the long laugh of neck touches the ground, the jaws close for good. You watch and wait for something else to happen, but nothing ever does. Nothing ever would. You could stand here watching for a hundred and fifty million years, Lord Claude, and nothing would ever happen here again. Gradually your bronto's mighty carcass, picked loving clean by predators, would sink into the slime, carried by its own weight deeper; then the waters would rise, and old Conqueror Sea come in with the leisurely air of a cardsharp dealing the boys a bad hand. Silt and sediment would filter down over the mighty grave, a slow rain with centuries to rain in. Old bronto's bed might be raised up and then down again perhaps half a dozen times, gently enough not to disturb him, although by now the sedimentary rocks would be forming thick around him. Finally, when he was wrapped in a tomb finer than any Indian rajah ever boasted, the powers of the Earth would raise him high on their shoulders until, sleeping still, bronto would lie in a brow of the Rockies high above the

indecision 犹豫不决
sacred 神圣的
cloister 隐居地
ravage 破坏
pane 边缘
nictitating membrane（眼睛）瞬膜
cadaver 死尸
reptile 爬行动物
flank 侧面
quaff 痛饮
beaker 无柄杯，烧杯
slay 屠杀 (slay, slew, slain)
carcass 尸体
cardsharp 赌徒
silt 泥沙
sediment 沉积
filter down 渗透
sedimentary 沉积的
rajah 首长
brow 顶峰

waters of the Pacific. But little any of that would count with you, Claude the Sword; once the **midget maggot** of life is dead in the creature's skull, the rest is no concern of yours.

7 You have no emotion now. You are just ***faintly** put out. You expected dramatic **thrashing** of the ground, or **bellowing**; on the other hand, you are glad the thing did not appear to suffer. You are like all cruel men, ***sentimental**; you are like all sentimental men, **squeamish**. You tuck the gun under your arm and walk round the dinosaur to view your victory.

8 You **prowl** past the **ungainly** hooves, round the **septic** white of the cliff of belly, beyond the **glistening** and how-thought-provoking cavern of the **cloaca**, finally posing beneath the switch-back sweep of tail-to-rump. Now your disappointment is as **crisp** and obvious as a visiting card: the giant is not half as big as you thought it was. It is not one half as large, for example, as the image of you and Maude is in your mind. Poor little warrior, science will never invent anything to assist the **titanic** death you want in the **contraterrene** caverns of your **fee-fi-fo fumblingly** fearful id!

9 Nothing is left to you now but to slink back to your time-mobile with a belly full of ***anticlimax**. See, the bright dung-consuming birds have already **cottoned on to** the true state of affairs; one by one, they gather up their hunched wings and fly **disconsolately** off across the swamp to other hosts. They know when a good thing turns bad, and do not wait for the **vultures** to drive them off; all hopes abandon, yes who **entrails** here. You also turn away.

10 You turn, but you pause. Nothing is left but to go back, no, but 2181 AD is not just the home date; it is Maude. It is Claude. It is the whole awful, hopeless, endless business of trying to adjust to an over-complex environment, of trying to turn yourself into a **cog**. Your escape from it into the Grand ***Simplicities** of the

midget 极小的
maggot 蛆
faintly 虚弱地
thrash 抽打，剧烈扭动
bellow 吼叫
sentimental 多愁善感的
squeamish 神经脆弱的
prowl 徘徊
ungainly 不堪入目的
septic 腐败的，感染的
glistening 闪光的
cloaca 泄殖腔
crisp 脆的
titanic 巨大的
contraterrene 非地球上的
fee-fi-fo 重复音节，强调威胁存在时的紧张
fumblingly 笨拙地，手忙脚乱地
anticlimax 扫兴；反高潮
cotton on to 明白，意识到
disconsolately 悲伤地
vulture 秃鹫
entrail 留下
cog 平庸的小人物
simplicity 纯朴

Jurassic, to quote the brochure again, was only a partial escape, now over.

11 So you pause, and as you pause, something lands **socko** on your back, pitching your face forward into tasty mud. You struggle and scream as lobster claws tear at your neck and throat. You try to pick up the rifle but cannot, so in agony you roll over, and next second the crab-thing is **greedying** it on your chest. You **wrench** at its shell, but it **giggles** and pecks your fingers off. You forgot when you killed the bronto that its parasites would leave it, and that to a little shrimp like you they would be a deal more dangerous than their hosts.

socko（俚语）令人震撼的表现
greedy 贪婪的
wrench 猛击
giggle 咯咯笑

Developing Ideas

Task Work in groups and discuss the following questions.

1. Is hunting a brontosaurus an easy task?
2. Did Claude Ford kill the brontosaurus?
3. After witnessing all of this, what were Claude's feelings?
4. Why did Claude feel disappointed?
5. How to understand the title *Poor Little Warrior*?

Using Language

Task 1 Learn the word formation from the table. Complete the sentences with the correct form of the words in the table.

Word	Prefix	Root	Suffix
rimless	/	rim 边缘	+less 否定后缀
intermittently	inter 两者之间	mitt 放开	+ent 形容词缀 +ly 副词缀
resistant	re- 回，反对	sist 站立	+ant 形容词缀

Word	Prefix	Root	Suffix
anticlimax	anti- 反对，抗议	climax 高潮	/
sentimental	/	sent 感觉	+ment 名词缀 +al 形容词缀
titanic	/	titan 巨大	+ic 形容词缀

1. Among the guests was a quiet, agreeable man with ____________ glasses looking like a college professor.
2. Everyone knows that if battery-powered devices are used ____________ they will consume more energy.
3. He made a lifelong contribution to breeding crops which are ____________ to pests and diseases.
4. The performance was fine in the first act, but the rest of the play was a(n) ____________.
5. The photo album wasn't worth very much but it had great ____________ value.
6. The world had witnessed a ____________ struggle between two visions of the future.

Task 2 Complete sentences with the correct form of the words in the box.

indecision	sacred	faintly	simplicity
insanely	groan	slay	destine

1. It was ____________ stressful work, done among people he didn't particularly like.
2. Now that darkness was falling, only their houses were outlined against the ____________ glimmering sky.
3. As a recent study has shown, too many choices can make us confused, unhappy — even paralyzed with ____________.
4. Students with such a growth mind-set were ____________ for greater academic success and were quite likely to outperform their counterparts.
5. Police warned the tourists about their safety because several visitors were brutally ____________ yesterday.
6. Hindu say the site is ____________ to them as the birthplace of Lord Ram and a temple has to be built there.
7. The beauty of the design lies in ____________ and elegance without any fancy decorations.
8. We all moan and ____________ about the loss of the quality of life through the destruction of our ecology.

Task 3　Translate the paragraph into Chinese.

China has launched its ecological environment satellite monitoring system, according to the China Academy of Space Technology (CAST). The system is also a satellite constellation of gross ecosystem product (GEP), which refers to the total value contributed by the ecosystem to human welfare and sustainable economic and social development. The ecological environment satellite monitoring system provides a variety of spatial basic data such as ecological classification, water conservation, atmospheric monitoring and carbon sink monitoring, to meet the demand for remote sensing data. (From Xinhua News Agency, 2023-04-12)

Part 3

Watching, Listening and Doing

Watching and Doing

Task 1 Scan the QR code to watch the video clip "The Story of the Nebula Awards (Ⅰ)" and fill in the blanks.

SCAN ME!

The Nebula Awards, presented by the Science Fiction and Fantasy Writers of America (SFWA), are a highly [1]____________ set of awards recognizing excellence in science fiction and fantasy literature.

Established in [2]____________, the Nebula Awards have become one of the most [3]____________ honors in the genre, celebrating outstanding works and contributions from both established and emerging authors.

The Nebula Awards encompass various [4]____________, including Best Novel, Best Novella, Best Novelette, Best Short Story, and the Andre Norton Award for Young Adult Science Fiction and Fantasy.

The selection process [5]____________ active members of SFWA nominating and voting for their favorite works from the previous year. This democratic [6]____________ ensures that the winners are chosen by their peers, adding to the significance of the award.

Over the years, the Nebula Awards have recognized [7]____________ works such as Ursula K. Le Guin's *The Left Hand of Darkness* and Isaac Asimov's *Foundation* series, as well as [8]____________ masterpieces like N.K. Jemisin's *The Fifth* Season. The awards not only honor exceptional storytelling but also contribute to the ongoing conversations within the science fiction and fantasy communities.

Task 2 Scan the QR code to watch the video clip "The Story of the Nebula Awards (Ⅱ)" and fill in the blanks.

SCAN ME!

The Nebula Awards are a testament to the vibrancy and [1]____________ of the science fiction and fantasy genres. The winners' list boasts a wide array of themes, styles, and [2]____________, showcasing the genre's ability to explore limitless possibilities. From space opera and dystopian futures to epic fantasies and alternate histories, the Nebula Awards celebrate the genre's ability to [3]____________ boundaries and challenge the imagination.

The Andre Norton Award for Young Adult Science Fiction and Fantasy recognizes the importance of nurturing young readers' love for [4]____________ fiction. By acknowledging outstanding works in this category, the Nebula Awards [5]____________ the growth of the genre by inspiring the next generation of writers and readers.

Beyond the individual awards, the Nebula Awards also highlight the [6]____________ nature of storytelling. The Best Dramatic Presentation category acknowledges the impact of science fiction and fantasy in other mediums, such as film and television. This recognition [7]____________ the genre's influence on popular culture and its ability to captivate audiences across various platforms.

The Nebula Conference, which accompanies the awards ceremony, [8]____________ a hub for discussions on the craft and business of writing. Panels, workshops, and presentations cover [9]____________ topics, from world-building techniques and character development to [10]____________ the publishing industry in the digital age. This rich exchange of knowledge benefits both [11]____________ and seasoned authors, fostering a sense of community and shared passion.

Winning a Nebula Award not only provides authors with a tangible accolade but also offers [12]____________ to a wider audience. The recognition often [13]____________ increased visibility, opening doors to new opportunities and collaborations within the literary world. The awards have played a pivotal role in [14]____________ science fiction and fantasy to a place of prominence within contemporary literature.

Listening and Doing

Task ***Scan the QR code to listen to the audio clip "Time Travel" and decide whether the statements are true (T) or false (F).***

SCAN ME!

1. Time travel is only a concept found in literature and films, and it has no basis in scientific discussions.
2. The "grandfather paradox" explores the potential consequences of traveling back in time and preventing one's own grandparents from meeting.
3. H. G. Wells' *The Time Machine* is a modern science fiction classic that explores the intricacies of time travel.
4. Einstein's theory of relativity suggests that time dilation can occur due to factors like speed and gravity.
5. Time travel is a concept that has been fully understood and explained by scientists, leaving little room for further debate or exploration.

Further Reading

Mini-Pedia — Winners of the Nebula Award

Harlan Ellison (1934-2018) was a prominent American writer known for his prolific and influential contributions to speculative fiction. Born on May 27, 1934, in Cleveland, Ohio, Ellison began his literary career in the 1950s, gaining recognition for his unique storytelling style that blended science fiction, fantasy, and social commentary.

Throughout his career, Ellison authored numerous short stories, novels, essays, and screenplays that explored a wide range of themes, from human nature to the complexities of the human condition. He was known for his sharp wit, thought-provoking narratives, and often controversial viewpoints.

Ellison's work received widespread acclaim, earning him multiple awards, including several prestigious Hugo, Nebula, and Edgar Awards. His famous short story *I Have No Mouth, and I Must Scream* is considered a classic of science fiction literature. He also contributed to the original *Star Trek* television series, penning the acclaimed episode *The City on the Edge of Forever*.

Roger Zelazny (1937-1995), born on May 13, 1937, in Euclid, Ohio, was a prominent American author known for his innovative contributions to science fiction and fantasy literature. He gained widespread recognition with his *Amber* series, which showcased his talent for blending intricate world-building, mythological themes, and complex characters. Zelazny's unique narrative style often featured poetic language and vivid imagery, setting him apart in the genre.

His literary achievements included winning multiple prestigious awards, such as the Hugo, Nebula, and Locus Awards. Zelazny's works, including the acclaimed novel *Lord of Light*, earned him a devoted following among both readers and fellow writers. His exploration of diverse themes, ranging from mythology to existentialism, added depth to his storytelling.

Tragically, Zelazny's life was cut short when he passed away on June 14, 1995, in Santa Fe, New Mexico. Despite his untimely death, his legacy endures through his influential body of work and the lasting impact he made on the speculative fiction genre.

Answer

Unit 8

Greg Bear and His Biotechnology

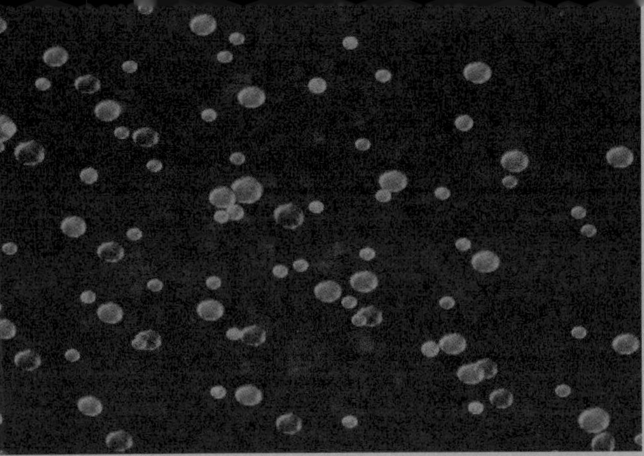
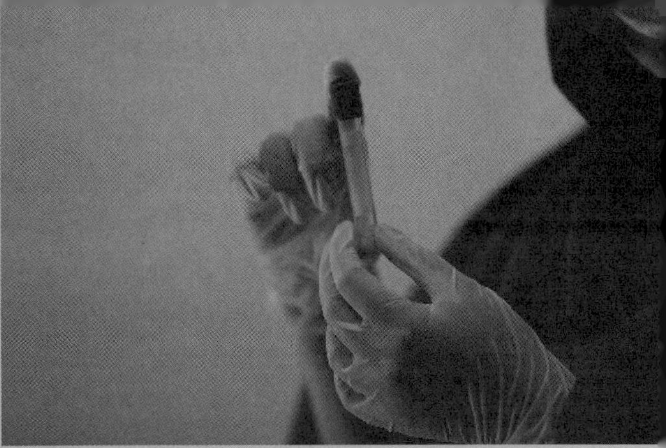

Starting out

Look at the pictures and discuss the following questions.

1. Have you ever thought about the tiny effect of all little live things — bacteria, microbes, "animalcules"?
2. Do you think it is possible for cells to become as smart as you and me or even smarter?
3. Can you imagine a person being totally controlled by his or her own cells?
4. How to deal with the relationship between all little live things — bacteria, microbes, "animalcules" and human beings?
5. If there was music in the blood, what would it sound like?

Part 1

Reading and Understanding

Blood Music (Ⅰ)

1 There is a principle in nature I don't think anyone has *pointed out before. Each hour, a myriad of trillions of little live things — bacteria, microbes, "animalcules" — are born and die, not counting for much except in the bulk of their existence and the accumulation of their tiny effects. They do not *perceive deeply. They don't suffer much. A hundred billion, dying, would not begin to have the same importance as a single human death.

2 Within the ranks of magnitude of all creatures, small as microbes or great as humans, there is an equality of "elan", just as the branches of a tall tree, gathered together, equal the bulk of the limbs below, and all the limbs equal the bulk of the trunk.

3 That, at least, is the principle. I believe Vergil Ulam was the first to *violate it.

4 It had been two years since I'd last seen Vergil. My memory of him hardly matched the tan, smiling, well-dressed gentleman standing before me. We had made a lunch appointment over the phone the day before, and now faced each other in the wide double doors of the employee's cafeteria at the Mount Freedom Medical Center.

5 "Vergil?" I asked. "My God, Vergil!"

6 "Good to see you, Edward." He shook my hand firmly. He had lost ten or twelve kilos and what remained seemed tighter, better proportioned. At the university, Vergil had been the pudgy, shock-haired, snaggle-toothed whiz kid who hot-wired doorknobs, gave us punch that turned our piss blue, and never got a date except with Eileen Termagent, who shared many of his physical characteristics.

7 "You look fantastic," I said. "Spend a summer in Cabo San

point out 指出
myriad 无数的
animalcule 微生物
perceive 感知，感觉
magnitude 数量，数值
elan 活力，热忱
violate 违反，违背
tan 棕褐色的
well-dressed 穿着讲究的
pudgy 肥胖的，胖墩墩的
snaggle-toothed 有凸牙的
whiz 奇才
hot-wire 热线发动，短路点火（不用钥匙而用电线短路方法发动汽车）
punch 潘趣酒
piss 尿，小便

Lucas?"

8 We stood in line at the counter and chose our food. "The tan," he said, *picking out a carton of chocolate milk, "is from spending three months under a sun lamp. My teeth were *straightened just after I last saw you. I'll explain the rest, but we need a place to talk where no one will listen close."

9 I steered him to the smokers' corner, where three die-hard puffers were scattered among six tables.

10 "Listen, I mean it," I said as we unloaded our trays. "You've changed. You're looking good."

11 "I've changed more than you know." His tone was motion-picture ominous, and he delivered the line with a *theatrical lift of his brows. "How's Gail?"

12 Gail was doing well, I told him, teaching nursery school. We'd married the year before. His gaze shifted down to his food — pineapple slice and cottage cheese, piece of banana cream pie — and he said, his voice almost cracking, "Notice something else?"

13 I squinted in *concentration. "Uh."

14 "Look closer."

15 "I'm not sure. Well, yes, you're not wearing glasses. "Contacts?"

16 "No. I don't need them anymore."

17 "And you're a *snappy dresser. Who's dressing you now? I hope she's as sexy as she is *tasteful."

18 "Candice isn't — wasn't — responsible for the improvements in my clothes," he said. "I just got a better job, more money to throw around. My taste in clothes is better than my taste in food, as it happens." He grinned the old Vergil self-deprecating grin, but ended it with a peculiar leer. "At any rate, she's left me, I've been fired from my job, I'm living on savings."

19 "Hold it," I said. "That's a bit crowded. Why not do a linear break-down? You got a job. Where?"

pick out 挑出
straighten （使）变直
steer 引导，带领
die-hard puffers 不抽烟就会死的重度烟民
ominous 不祥的，不吉利的
theatrical 夸张的，戏剧性的
crack （突然）变嘶哑，变沙哑
squint 眯着眼睛看
concentration 专心，专注
contacts 隐形眼镜
snappy 时髦的
tasteful 有品位的
self-deprecating 自谦的
leer 一瞥，斜睨
at any rate 不管怎样
linear （过程或发展）线性的
break-down 分解

20 "Genetron Corp.," he said. "Sixteen months ago."

21 "I haven't heard of them."

22 "You will. They're putting out common stock in the next month. It'll **shoot off the board**. They've *__broken through__* with MABs. Medical — "

23 "I know what MABs are," I interrupted. "At least in theory. Medically Applicable Biochips."

24 "They have some that work."

25 "What?" It was my turn to **lift my brows**.

26 "**Microscopic** logic circuits. You inject them into the human body, they set up shop where they're told and **troubleshoot**. With Dr Michael Bernard's approval."

27 That was quite impressive. Bernard's reputation was **spotless**. Not only was he *__associated with__* the **genetic engineering** biggies, but he had made news at least once a year in his practice as a **neurosurgeon** before retiring. Covers on *Time, Mega, Rolling Stone.

28 "That's supposed to be secret — stock, breakthrough, Bernard, everything." He looked around and lowered his voice. "But you do whatever the hell you want. I'm through with the **bastards**."

29 I **whistled**. "Make me rich, huh?"

30 "If that's what you want. Or you can spend some time with me before rushing off to your broker."

31 "Of course." He hadn't touched the cottage cheese or pie. He had, however, eaten the pineapple slice and drunk the chocolate milk. "So tell me more."

32 "Well, in med school I was training for lab work. Biochemical research. I've always *__had a bent for__* computers, too. So I put myself through my last two years — "

33 "By selling software packages to Westinghouse," I said.

34 "It's good my friends remember. That's how I *__got involved__*

shoot off the board (股价)一飞冲天
break through 突破
lift one's brows 皱起眉头
microscopic 微观的
troubleshoot 解决问题
spotless 没有污点的
be associated with 和……来往
genetic engineering 遗传工程(学)
neurosurgeon 神经外科医师
bastard 杂种,浑蛋,恶棍
whistle 吹口哨
have a bent for 有(某方面的)天赋,爱好
get involved with 参与

with Genetron, just when they were starting out. They had big money backers, all the lab facilities I thought anyone would ever need. They hired me, and I advanced rapidly."

35 "Four months and I was doing my own work. I made some breakthroughs," he tossed his hand *nonchalantly, "then I *went off on tangents they thought were premature. I persisted and they took away my lab, handed it over to a certifiable flatworm. I managed to save part of the experiment before they fired me. But I haven't exactly been cautious ... or judicious. So now it's going on outside the lab."

36 I'd always regarded Vergil as ambitious, a trifle cracked, and not terribly sensitive. His relations with authority figures had never been smooth. Science, for him, was like the woman you couldn't possibly have, who suddenly opens her arms to you, long before you're ready for mature love — leaving you afraid you'll forever blow the chance, lose the prize, screw up royally. Apparently, he had. "Outside the lab? I don't get you."

37 "Edward, I want you to examine me. Give me a *thorough physical. Maybe a cancer diagnostic. Then I'll explain more."

38 "You want a five-thousand-dollar exam?"

39 "Whatever you can do. Ultrasound, NMR, thermogram, everything."

40 "I don't know if I can *get access to all that equipment. NMR full-scan has only been here a month or two. Hell, you couldn't pick a more expensive way — "

41 "Then ultrasound. That's all you'll need."

42 "Vergil, I'm an obstetrician, not a glamour-boy lab-tech. OB-GYN, butt of all jokes. If you're turning into a woman, maybe I can help you."

43 He leaned forward, almost putting his elbow into the pie, but swinging wide at the last instant by scant millimeters. The old Vergil would have hit it square. "Examine me closely and

facility 设施，设备
nonchalantly 漫不经心地
go off on a tangent 突然背离原来的思路
certifiable 愚蠢透顶的
flatworm 扁虫
judicious 明断的
cracked 疯狂的
screw up 搞糟，搅乱
royally 极度地
thorough 彻底的，完全的
Ultrasound 超声波扫描检查
NMR(Nuclear Magnetic Resonance) 核磁共振
thermogram 温度记录图
get access to 使用
obstetrician 产科医生
OB-GYN (Obstetrics and Gynaecology) 妇产科（学），妇产科医生
butt（嘲弄等的）对象，笑柄
scant 微小的，不足的
hit it square 直接碰上去，直击要害

you'll …" He narrowed his eyes and shook his head. "Just examine me."

44 "So I make an appointment for ultrasound. Who's going to pay?"

45 "I'm on Blue Shield." He smiled and held up a medical credit card. "I **messed with** the personnel files at Genetron. Anything up to a hundred thousand dollars medical, they'll never check, never suspect."

mess with 干预，干扰

Developing Ideas

Task 1 Summarize the story and complete the table.

PARAS 1-3	There is a principle in nature. And I believe Vergil Ulam [1] ____________.
PARAS 4-18	Vergil has changed a lot since I had last seen him two years ago. ● He had turned into a [2] ____________ gentleman. ● He had lost ten or twelve kilos and what remained seemed [3] ____________. ● His teeth were [4] ____________. ● He is not [5] ____________.
PARAS 19-36	The reason why Vergil has been fired from his job: ● Vergil got a job in Genetron sixteen months ago. They had [6] ____________, [7] ____________ he thought anyone would ever need. ● Vergil [8] ____________ in his work, but then he [9] ____________ Genetron thought were [10] ____________.
PARAS 37-45	Vergil wants me to [11] ____________, then he'll explain more. *Guess what would Vergil go off to? What does "So now it's going on outside the lab" mean? And what consequence would this bring about?

Task 2 Decide whether the statements are true (T) or false (F) according to the passage.

1. A hundred billion microbes dying would not have the same importance as a single human death.
2. People pay much attention to trillions of little live things because of the bulk of their existence and the accumulation of their tiny effects.
3. I didn't like Vergil back at the university, because he had been the pudgy, shock-haired, snaggle-toothed whiz kid who hot-wired doorknobs, gave us punch that turned our piss blue.
4. Vergil has become a snappy dresser, because Candice is dressing him now.
5. Vergil is such an ambitious, crazy genius, but he can't handle his relations with authority figures well.
6. Vergil failed to save his experiment, because he was so careless.

Using Language

Task 1 Complete the table with the correct form of the words given. Then complete the sentences with the correct form of the words in the table.

Verb	Noun	Adjective	Adverb
perceive			
violate			
straighten			
		ominous	
		theatrical	
		tasteful	
	concentration		
		thorough	
			nonchalantly
		snappy	

1. The road twisted its way up the mountain then ____________ out for the last two hundred yards.
2. To the disappointment of fans, the final scene was terribly lacking in ____________ effect.
3. He spoke ____________ of the world facing a war in Europe and possibly something worse.
4. Some tasks that require unbroken ____________ for long periods can often be done more smoothly from home than in open-plan offices.
5. John is quite a fashionable guy. He always dresses pretty ____________.
6. Health experts agree that you should wash your hands regularly and ____________ as well with soap and water for at least 20 seconds.
7. It is the biggest penalty imposed by the European Union on a company for privacy ____________.
8. The ____________ of colour mainly occurs inside our heads and so is subjective and prone to personal experience.
9. They come in red and green varieties; the red has an earthly floral ____________, while the green is slightly bitter but fresh.
10. He appeared ____________ in court even when the judge ordered him to pay $10,000.

Task 2 Complete the sentences with the correct form of the phrases in the box.

point out	pick out	break through	go off on a tangent
associate with	have a bent for	get involved with	get access to

1. An urban farmer made full use of the livestreaming to help people ____________ locally grown food.
2. My mother doesn't allow me to ____________ the bad kids in our community.
3. ____________ natural history directed him towards his first job.
4. It's natural to ____________ when you're nervous, and that couldn't be truer in the interview room.
5. He ____________ that many candy and snack companies have changed their formulas when selling their products in Europe.
6. As online voting becomes increasingly popular, people can ____________ many competitions.
7. Scientists think they are beginning to ____________ in the fight against cancer.
8. The pair were constantly in competition throughout their childhoods, whether that was their performance in school or their abilities to ____________ the best Mother's Day gift.

Task 3 Translate the sentences into Chinese.

1. Within the ranks of magnitude of all creatures, small as microbes or great as humans, there is an equality of "elan", just as the branches of a tall tree, gathered together, equal the bulk of the limbs below, and all the limbs equal the bulk of the trunk.

____

____

____

2. At the university, Vergil had been the pudgy, shock-haired, snaggle-toothed whiz kid who hot-wired doorknobs, gave us punch that turned our piss blue, and never got a date except with Eileen Termagent, who shared many of his physical characteristics.

____

____

____

Task 4 Translate the paragraph into English.

近十年来中国在生物制药领域取得了显著的突破。首先,中国加大了对科研和技术创新的投入,推动了新药研发。其次,中国成功应用基因编辑技术,为精准医学的发展提供了强有力的支持。此外,中国在疫苗研发和生产领域也取得了重要突破。中国的生物制药公司开发出了多种高效安全的疫苗,有效应对了疫苗需求的增长以及全球公共卫生挑战。

Part 2

Appreciating and Comprehending

Blood Music (II)

1 "Then I really went off on my own. We had the equipment, the techniques; and I knew the **molecular** language. I could make really dense, really complicated biochips by ***compounding** the **nucleoproteins**, making them into little brains. I did some research into how far I could go, **theoretically**. Sticking with bacteria, I could make them a biochip with the computing capacity of a sparrow's brain. Imagine how **jazzed** I was! Then I saw a way to increase the ***complexity** a **thousandfold**, by using something we regarded as a **nuisance** — **quantum** chitchat between the fixed elements of the **circuits**. Down that small, even the slightest change could bomb a biochip. But I developed a program that actually predicted and took advantage of **electron tunneling**. Emphasized the **heuristic** aspects of the computer, used the chitchat as a method of increasing complexity."

2 "You're losing me," I said.

3 "I took advantage of **randomness**. The circuits could repair themselves, compare memories, and correct faulty elements. The whole **schmeer**. I gave them basic instructions: Go forth and multiply. Improve. By God, you should have seen some of the **cultures** a week later! It was amazing. They were ***evolving** all on their own, like little cities. I destroyed them all. I think one of the **petri dishes** would have grown legs and walked out of the **incubator** if I'd kept feeding it."

4 "You're kidding." I looked at him. "You' re not kidding."

5 "Man, they knew what it was like to improve! They knew where they had to go, but they were just so limited, being in bacteria bodies, with so few resources."

6 "How smart were they?"

molecular 分子的
compound 使合成，结合
nucleoprotein 核蛋白
theoretically 理论上
jazzed 激动的，兴奋的
complexity 复杂性
thousandfold 千倍的
nuisance 麻烦事
quantum 量子
circuit 电路，线路
electron tunneling 电子隧道效应
heuristic（计算机程序）探试的，探索的
randomness 随意，随机
schmeer 事情
culture 培养菌
evolve 进化
petri dish 皮氏培养皿（作细菌等培养用的有盖玻璃碟）
incubator 恒温器（用于培养细菌等）

7 "I couldn't be sure. They were associating **in clusters** of a hundred to two hundred cells, each cluster behaving like an **autonomous** unit. Each cluster might have been as smart as a **rhesus monkey**. They exchanged information through their **pili**, passed on bits of memory, and compared notes. Their organization was obviously different from a group of monkeys. Their world was so much simpler, for one thing. With their abilities, they were masters of the petri dishes. I put phages in with them; the **phages** didn't have a chance. They used every option available to change and grow."

8 "How is that possible?"

9 "What?" He seemed surprised I wasn't **accepting** everything **at face value**.

10 "***Cramming** so much into so little. A rhesus monkey is not your simple little calculator, Vergil."

11 "I haven't made myself clear," he said, obviously ***irritated**. "I was using nucleoprotein computers. They're like DNA, but all the information can ***interact**. Do you know how many **nucleotide pairs** there are in the DNA of a single bacteria?"

12 It had been a long time since my last biochemistry lesson. I shook my head.

13 "About two million. Add in the ***modified ribosome structures** — fifteen thousand of them, each with a molecular weight of about three million — and consider the combinations and ***permutations**. The RNA is arranged like a ***continuous** loop paper tape, surrounded by ribosomes ticking off instructions and manufacturing protein chains ..." His eyes were bright and slightly moist. Besides, "I'm not saying every cell was a ***distinct entity**. They cooperated."

14 "How many bacteria in the dishes you destroyed?"

15 "Billions. I don't know." He **smirked**. "You got it, Edward. Whole **planetsful** of **E. coli**."

in clusters of 成团
autonomous 独立自主的
rhesus monkey 恒河猴
pili 菌毛
phage 噬菌体
accept ... at face value 不质疑，不怀疑就相信（某事）
cram 把……塞进，挤满
irritated 恼怒的，生气的
interact 互动
nucleotide pair 核苷酸对
modified 经过调整的
ribosome structure 核糖体结构
permutation 排列，置换
continuous 持续的
distinct 不同的
entity 独立存在物
smirk 自鸣得意地笑
planetsful 是作者自己造的词，此处可理解为"好几个星球的"
E. coli 大肠杆菌

16 "But they didn't fire you then?"

17 "No. They didn't know what was going on, for one thing. I kept compounding the molecules, increasing their size and complexity. When bacteria were too limited, I took blood from myself, separated out white cells, and injected them with the new biochips. I watched them, put them through **mazes** and little chemical problems. They were whizzes. Time is a lot faster at that level — so little distance for the messages to cross, and the environment is much simpler. Then I forgot to store a file under my **secret code** in the lab computers. Some managers found it and guessed what I was **up to**. Everybody **panicked**. They thought we'd have every **social watchdog** in the country on our backs because of what I'd done. They started to destroy my work and wipe my programs. Ordered me to ⋆**sterilize** my white cells. Christ." He pulled the white robe off and started to get dressed. "I only had a day or two. I separated out the most complex cells — "

18 "How complex?"

19 "They were clustering in hundred-cell groups, like the bacteria. Each group as smart as a ten-year-old kid, maybe." He studied my face for a moment. "Still doubting? Want me to run through how many nucleotide pairs there are in a **mammalian cell**? I ⋆**tailored** my computers to take advantage of the white cells' capacity. Ten billion nucleotide pairs, Edward. Ten E-f-ing ten. And they don't have a huge body to worry about, taking up most of their thinking time."

20 "Okay," I said. "I'm ⋆**convinced**. What did you do?"

21 "I mixed the cells back into a **cylinder** of whole blood and injected myself with it." He buttoned the top of his shirt and smiled **thinly** at me. "I'd programmed them with every drive I could, talked as high a level as I could using just **enzymes** and such. After that, they were on their own."

maze 迷宫
secret code 密码
up to 从事，忙于
panick 惊慌失措
social watchdog 社会监察机构
sterilize 使绝育；使不起作用
mammalian cell 哺乳动物细胞
tailor 量身定做
convince 使信服
cylinder（尤指用作容器的）圆筒状物
thinly 冷淡地
enzyme 酶

22 "You programmed them to go forth and *multiply, improve?" I repeated.

23 "I think they developed some characteristics picked up by the biochips in their E. coli phases. The white cells could talk to one another with extruded memories. They almost certainly found ways to ingest other types of cells and alter them without killing them."

24 "You're crazy."

25 …

26 His smile vanished. "But then one night my skin started to crawl. It really scared me. I thought things were getting out of hand. I wondered what they'd do when they crossed the blood-brain barrier and found out about me — about the brain's real function. So I began a campaign to keep them under control. I figured, the reason they wanted to get into the skin was the simplicity of running circuits across a surface. Much easier than trying to maintain chains of communication in and around muscles, organs, vessels. The skin was much more direct. So I bought a quartz lamp." He caught my puzzled expression. "In the lab, we'd break down the protein in biochip cells by *exposing them to ultraviolet light. I *alternated sun lamp with quartz treatments. Keeps them out of my skin, so far as I can tell, and gives me a nice tan."

27 "Give you skin cancer, too," I commented.

28 "They'll probably take care of that. Like police."

29 "Okay, I've examined you, you've told me a story I still find hard to believe ... what do you want me to do?"

multiply (使)繁殖
extrude 喷出，释放
ingest 吸收
crawl 爬
figure 认为，认定（某事将发生或属实）
vessel 血管
quartz lamp 石英灯
expose 使暴露
ultraviolet light 紫外线灯
alternate 使交替

Developing Ideas

Task Work in groups and discuss the following questions.

1. What did Vergil go off to?
2. Why did Vergil think he would control those complicated biochips he made in the first place?
3. What were the unique features of the complex cells?
4. What does "So now it's going on outside the lab" in Part 1 mean?
5. Why did Vergil want to take a thorough physical exam?
6. Can you imagine what consequence it would bring about, if Vergil couldn't control those cells?
7. What do you think of Vergil from Part 2?

Using Language

Task 1 Learn the word formation from the table. Complete the sentences with the correct form of the words in the table.

Word	Prefix	Root	Suffix
modify	/	mod=mode, manner 方式，模式	+ify 使……，动词缀
compound	com- 加强	pound=to put, to place 放，放置	/
sterilize	/	steril 无菌的	+ize ……化，动词缀
interact	inter- 相互	act=to do, to drive 做，驱使	/
evolve	e- 向外，离开	volv 卷，转	+e 结构性后缀
permutation	per- 贯穿，全部	mut 改变	+ation 名词缀
continuous	con- 共同	tin 握，持有	+uous 具有……性质的，形容词缀
expose	ex- 出，外	pos 放，摆	+e 结构性后缀

1. The software we use has been ____________ to provide better service for us.
2. It is unique because its particular ____________ of genes has not appeared before.

3. All employees who had a record of five years' ____________ employment with the firm will get a pay rise this year.
4. Honey is basically a ____________ of water, two types of sugar, vitamins and enzymes.
5. This behavior may have ____________ as dogs gradually learned they could benefit from avoiding conflicts with humans.
6. Scientists are trying to find out the ____________ of bacteria with the body's natural chemistry.
7. The eruption completely ____________ the island, but just months later, life began to flourish again.
8. The broken windows left us ____________ to the sub-zero temperatures.

Task 2 Complete the sentences with the correct form of the words in the box.

alternate	complexity	convince	multiply
tailor	irritate	distinct	cram

1. She ____________ in watching the clock and staring at the telephone, waiting for her boyfriend to call her.
2. It's too late to call a car, so five of us all have to ____________ into his car.
3. The way she spoils her children really ____________ me, but she never changes that.
4. The increasing ____________ of modern telecommunication systems is not friendly to old people.
5. I cannot ____________ myself that she is dead, because I just talked to her yesterday.
6. A moist tea towel left in a warm kitchen provides an ideal environment for bacteria to ____________.
7. Every city wants to have its own landmark that gives it a sense of ____________ culture.
8. Most travel agents are prepared to ____________ travel arrangements to meet individual requirements.

Task 3 Translate the paragraph into Chinese.

The introduction of hybrid rice, a remarkable achievement in agricultural biotechnology, has revolutionized rice cultivation and played a pivotal role in ensuring global food security. Hybrid rice combines the advantageous traits from two genetically distinct rice varieties, resulting in higher yields, disease resistance, and improved grain quality. In China, the development of hybrid rice has been particularly noteworthy. The pioneering work of Chinese scientists, such as the "father of hybrid rice" Yuan Longping, has led to significant advancements in this field. Through careful crossbreeding and selection, they have successfully created hybrid rice varieties with exceptional performance, exceeding the productivity of traditional rice varieties.

Part 3

Watching, Listening and Doing

Watching and Doing

Task 1 Scan the QR code to watch the video clip "The Life Story of Greg Bear (Ⅰ)" and fill in the blanks.

SCAN ME!

Greg Bear, born on August 20, 1951, in San Diego, California, is an [1]____________ American science fiction author renowned for his imaginative [2]____________ and in-depth exploration of scientific concepts. Throughout his career, Bear has [3]____________ a prominent place for himself in science fiction, earning numerous [4]____________ and applause.

As a child, Bear [5]____________ a passion for storytelling and writing. At the age of fifteen, he published his first short story, showing his [6]____________ and setting the stage for a successful literary career.

After graduating from high school, Bear [7]____________ at San Diego State University, where he pursued a degree in [8]____________. During his time at university, he delved deeper into various literary genres and explored the works of science fiction writers who would later influence his own writing style.

Bear's fascination with science and technology also took root during his college years. He [9]____________ himself in scientific literature, studying a wide range of subjects, including physics, biology, and computer science. This strong [10]____________ in science provided him with a solid understanding of scientific principles, which he incorporates well into his stories.

Task 2 Scan the QR code to watch the video clip "The Life Story of Greg Bear (Ⅱ)" and fill in the blanks.

SCAN ME!

One of Bear's most famous works is [1]____________, published in 1985. This novel explores the consequences of genetic engineering gone wrong and tries hard to find out the [2]____________ of consciousness.

Another [3]____________ work by Bear is *Eon*, published in 1985. This novel takes readers on a [4]____________ of discovery as a mysterious alien artifact(外星文物), the Stone, appears in Earth's [5]____________. The novel explores themes of time travel, [6]____________, and the evolution of mankind.

In 1999, Bear released *Darwin's Radio*, a [7]__________ novel that explores the consequences of an evolutionary event that causes rapid changes in human [8]__________. *Darwin's Radio* received [9]__________ acclaim(称赞) and won several big awards, including the Nebula Award for Best Novel(星云奖最佳小说奖).

Beyond his [10]__________ career as a novelist, Bear has also made great contributions to shared universes. He has written for the *Star Trek*(《星际迷航》) and *Halo*(《光环》) franchises (系列), [11]__________ upon these beloved worlds while filling them with his unique creativity and [12]__________.

Greg Bear's impact on science fiction is undeniable. With his brilliant ideas and deep understanding of scientific principles, he has [13]__________ generations of readers and fellow authors. His work has earned him huge achievements, including [14]__________ Hugo(雨果奖)and Nebula Awards, making him one of the most [15]__________ and influential authors in this field.

Today, Bear continues to write and [16]__________ audiences with his imaginative works. As a famous author within the science fiction community, his works will continue to [17]__________ the genre and inspire future writers to explore the [18]__________ possibilities of the human imagination.

Listening and Doing

SCAN ME!

***Task** Scan the QR code to listen to the audio clip "Artificial Intelligence" and decide whether the statements are true (T) or false (F).*

1. Intelligent machines are designed to perceive, understand, learn, reason, and make decisions similar to or even better than humans.
2. Intelligent machines need explicit programming to tell them how to learn from and adapt to data.
3. Machines can analyze and interpret visual information, but they can't read emotions as they have no feelings.
4. In healthcare, AI is being used to develop diagnostic systems, analyze medical images, except for surgery.
5. Researchers and policymakers are afraid that AI may be used to violate our privacy, and take our jobs.
6. Artificial General Intelligence (AGI) is the highest goal of AI research that aims to build machines that possess human-like intelligence across a wide range of tasks.

Further Reading

Mini-Pedia — Famous Chinese Science Fiction Writers

Liu Cixin (1963-) is a renowned Chinese science fiction writer and one of the most prominent Chinese science fiction authors in the world. Born in 1963 in Henan Province, China, he graduated from North China University of Water Resources and Electric Power. His works are highly regarded for their depth, innovation, and scientific plausibility.

Liu Cixin is best known for his acclaimed *Remembrance of Earth's Past* trilogy, with *The Three-Body Problem* as its centerpiece. This series has earned him international acclaim and a wide readership. It blends unique storytelling, vast imagination, and incorporates themes of science, philosophy, and societal issues. *The Three-Body Problem* became the first Chinese science fiction novel to win the prestigious Hugo Award, establishing an important milestone for Chinese science fiction in the global arena.

Regarded as one of the greatest contemporary science fiction writers, Liu Cixin's influence extends beyond the realm of science fiction. He is loved and respected by readers worldwide, and his works have not only brought joy and inspiration but also propelled the development and international exchange of Chinese science fiction.

Wang Jinkang (1948-), born on November 24, 1948, in Nanyang, Henan Province, is a senior engineer, a member of the China Writers Association, a member of the China Popular Science Writers Association, and a member of the Science and Literature Committee. To date, he has published 87 short stories and more than 10 novels, totaling over 5 million words.

He received the Galaxy Award at the 1997 International Science Fiction Conference and the Lifetime Achievement Award at the Global Chinese Science Fiction Nebula Awards. One of his representative works, *Seven Shells*, revolves around an advanced virtual reality technology. This technology enables people to enter a virtual world constructed from "seven shells", where they can escape the pressures and troubles of real life and experience a vibrant, diverse existence. However, the introduction of this technology comes with significant moral and societal challenges, gradually eroding people's genuine emotions and quality of life.

The protagonist is a technical expert working in this virtual world. Over time, he becomes increasingly aware of the detrimental effects of virtual life addiction on human identity. As the story unfolds, he faces a profound choice: to continue indulging in this fantastical world or to reexamine real life and rediscover his authentic self. The story not only explores the allure of the virtual world but also highlights humanity's fragility and confusion in the face of rapid technological advancement.

Answer